PRAISE

"Profound . . . The authors are engaging guides to their field."

—*Financial Times*

"Corralling a wealth of fascinating examples . . . Sharot and Sunstein provide a revelatory investigation of a phenomenon that's as complex as it is common. This enthralls."

—*Publishers Weekly* (starred review)

"With intelligence and humor, Sharot and Sunstein provide guidance on how to refresh the spirit and see the world anew. If your world is starting to look gray and dull, this book might be your road map out of the comfort zone."

—*Kirkus Reviews*

"*Look Again* is a worthy addition to literature at the intersection of psychology, neuroscience, and economics, making them accessible to the general reader."

—*Shelf Awareness*

"One trait of history's most creative thinkers—from Leonardo da Vinci to Albert Einstein—is that they are able to look anew and marvel at everyday things that most people have quit noticing: the alluring blueness of the sky, the passage of time, the way a light beam creates a spot of luster on a leaf. *Look Again* can help us all look in a fresh way at things around us. It's a smart and fun read, and a valuable way to revitalize your life."

—Walter Isaacson, *New York Times* bestselling author of *Steve Jobs*

"Timely and important. A clear and provocative book about the power of expectation and the endless mystery of the human mind."
—Tara Westover, #1 *New York Times* bestselling author of *Educated*

"A sensational guide to a more psychologically rich life."
—Angela Duckworth, *New York Times* bestselling author of *Grit*

"In *Look Again,* Sharot and Sunstein offer an insightful look into the science of habituation. Their insights into the why and how of getting used to things teach us how to hack habituation to bring more joy to our lives. A surprising and delightful book."
—Annie Duke, bestselling author of *Thinking in Bets*

"*Look Again* is the perfect book to help you refresh your point of view. Sharot and Sunstein reveal why it's easy to be lulled into complacency about anything and how to prevent falling into this trap. In the bargain, they'll help you live a happier, healthier, wiser, and more just life."
—Katy Milkman, bestselling author of *How to Change*

"Such a vivid, human, and original book—the perfect guide to perking up everything from your creativity to your love life."
—Tim Harford, author of *How to Make the World Add Up*

"*Look Again* is a fascinating guide to how and why our biased minds get used to stuff and how we can fight through our usual adaptations. It's a must-read for anyone who wants to feel happier, stay more present, and make healthier, more effective decisions."
—Laurie Santos, Chandrika and Ranjan Tandon Professor of Psychology at Yale University and host of *The Happiness Lab* podcast

LOOK AGAIN

THE POWER OF NOTICING
WHAT WAS ALWAYS THERE

Tali Sharot and
Cass R. Sunstein

ONE SIGNAL
PUBLISHERS

ATRIA

New York · Amsterdam/Antwerp · London · Toronto · Sydney · New Delhi

ONE SIGNAL
PUBLISHERS

ATRIA

An Imprint of Simon & Schuster, LLC
1230 Avenue of the Americas
New York, NY 10020

First One Signal Publishers/Atria Paperback edition January 2025

ONE SIGNAL PUBLISHERS / ATRIA PAPERBACK and colophon are trademarks of
Simon & Schuster, LLC.

For information about special discounts for bulk purchases, please contact Simon
& Schuster Special Sales at 1-866-506-1949 or business@simonandschuster.com.

The Simon & Schuster Speakers Bureau can bring authors to your live event. For
more information or to book an event, contact the Simon & Schuster Speakers
Bureau at 1-866-248-3049 or visit our website at www.simonspeakers.com.

Interior design by Dana Sloan

Manufactured in the United States of America

1   3   5   7   9   10   8   6   4   2

Library of Congress Cataloging-in-Publication Data is available.

ISBN 978-1-6680-0820-1
ISBN 978-1-6680-0821-8 (pbk)
ISBN 978-1-6680-0822-5 (ebook)

To Livia, Leo, Ellyn, Declan, and Rían

A thousand things that had seemed unnatural and repulsive speedily became natural and ordinary to me. I suppose everything in existence takes its colour from the average hue of our surroundings.

—H. G. Wells[1]

CONTENTS

Contents

LOOK AGAIN

INTRODUCTION:

HOW WE HABITUATE TO
EVERYTHING, ALL THE TIME

Habituation. It may be as fundamental a
characteristic of life as DNA.

—VINCENT GASTON DETHIER[1]

WHAT WAS THE BEST day of your life? You might find
it difficult to select the *very* best day. That's fine; just
choose a really good day.

Some people think back to their wedding day. Others choose
the day a child was born or their graduation day. Others give
more idiosyncratic answers: "The day I break-danced with my
Labrador Retriever on the roof" or "The day I gave a speech
about the fear of public speaking." As long as it was a great day,
it qualifies.

Envision reliving that day. The sun is out; the sky is blue; you
are running on the beach in your yellow bathing suit. Or maybe
the sky is dark; the snow is falling; you warm your red nose against

that of a newfound love. Whatever it is—it's joyful. Now imagine reliving that day. Again. And again. And again. And again. You are trapped in a "best day of my life" loop. What will happen?

What will happen is that the best day of your life will become less exciting, less joyful, less fun, and less meaningful. Soon the best day of your life will become tedious. The sun will not feel as warm, the snow not as magical, your love not so perfect, your accomplishments not as great, and your mentors not as wise.

What is thrilling on Monday becomes boring by Friday. We *habituate*, which means that we respond less and less to stimuli that repeat.[2] That's human nature. Even those things that you once found exhilarating (a relationship, a job, a song, a work of art) lose their sparkle after a while. Studies show that people even start habituating to the magic of a tropical vacation within forty-three hours of arrival.[3]

But what if you could restore your sense of amazement about those things that you no longer feel or notice? What if you could, to some extent, *dishabituate*?

That's what this book is about. We will ask what could happen if people were able to overcome habituation in the office, in the bedroom, or on the athletic field. What would be the impact on happiness, relationships, work, community? And how would you go about doing that? We will see how temporarily changing your environment, changing the rules, changing the people with whom you interact, and taking real or imagined mini-breaks from ordinary life can help you regain sensitivity and start noticing what you barely see.

We won't look only at how you can dishabituate to the best things, such as a terrific job, home, neighborhood, or relationship. We will also explore how you can dishabituate to the bad things. Now, you may think that is a dreadful idea. Why would you want to experience terrible things as if for the first time? If we made you experience the worst day of your life over and over and over, surely you would want a brain that habituates. You would want the pain of misery or heartache to weaken over time. That would be a blessing.

Fair enough, but here is the problem. When we habituate to the bad things, we are less motivated to strive for change. That Tuesday's nightmare is Sunday's snore becomes a serious challenge for fighting foolishness, cruelty, suffering, waste, corruption, discrimination, misinformation, and tyranny. Habituation to what is bad can lead us to take reckless financial risks, to fail to notice gradual changes in our children's behavior that should raise concerns, to allow faint cracks in our romantic relationships to grow larger and larger, and to stop being bothered by stupidity or inefficiency at work.

So we will explore what happens when you habituate not only to the good, but also to the bad, and how to dishabituate. We will travel to Sweden, where switching the side of the road on which people drive led to a temporary decrease of approximately 40 percent in accidents, partly because of risk dishabituation.[4] We will see how clean-air chambers may help people notice (and therefore care about) pollution, how stepping into someone else's shoes can help us dishabituate to discrimination,[5] and how taking breaks from social media can help you appreciate your life again.[6] We will examine how looking at things anew, or from the side, can produce startling innovation.

But before we dive into all that, let's consider *why* we are so quick to habituate to everything all the time. (Well, almost everything, and almost all the time. We'll get to that.) We will consider why we have evolved a brain that is wired to want things (a fancy car, a big house, a loving spouse, a high-paying job), but then quick to overlook those things when we finally get them. We will ask why, despite being sophisticated creatures, we are relatively quick to accept dreadful things that become the norm, such as cruelty, corruption, and discrimination. To resolve these puzzles, we will use ideas and work from psychology, neuroscience, economics, and philosophy— some from our own research, some from others'.

Why are we quick to habituate? The answer is not that we are weak, ungrateful, or overwhelmed beings who do not appreciate threats and wonders. The answer has to do with a basic characteristic that we, two-legged, big-headed creatures, share with every other animal on earth, including apes, dogs, birds, frogs, fish, rats, and even bacteria.

HOW IT STARTED . . . WHERE IT'S GOING

More than 3 billion years ago, your ancestors appeared on earth.[7] But you would not know it by looking at them. The resemblance is not apparent. They were smaller in size and less cultured. Fortunately, they were sophisticated enough to survive rough conditions. They did not have legs, but they could swim and tumble along in search of nutrient-rich environments. Yet even these primitive actions exhibited the hallmarks of habituation: when the level of nutrients in the environment was constant, your ancestors tumbled at a constant rate on a kind of autopilot. Only when the levels of nutrients changed did the frequency of their movements alter.[8]

Who were these early creatures? They were unicellular bacteria. As their name suggests, they were composed of only a single cell. In comparison, you have 37.2 trillion cells in your body.[9] These cells interact, enabling you not only to swim and tumble, but also to run, jump, laugh, sing, and shout. But the behavior of even a single cell can habituate by inhibiting its own response.

Many years after unicellular organisms appeared on earth, simple multicellular organisms emerged. These organisms have neurons that can "talk" to each other. The likelihood that they will talk changes over time. After one neuron sends an initial message to another neuron—perhaps a sensory neuron conveying information about a stinky odor to a motor neuron—it will often reduce the frequency of its signals even if the odor is still present.[10] As a result, behavioral responses, such as movements away from that odor, reduce.

These processes happen in the human brain too. This is one reason you may stop noticing the smell of tobacco after a few minutes in a smoke-filled room, and why you might be amazed to find yourself getting used to background noise that, at first, greatly irritated you.

To demonstrate this basic principle, let us go back in time to Vienna, Austria, in 1804. A twenty-four-year-old Swiss physician, Ignaz Paul Vital Troxler, was studying vision when he made an astonishing discovery.[11] He noticed that if he fixed his eyes on an image for long enough at close distance, it seemed to disappear. Try it yourself. Locate the colorful image on the back cover of this book (it is a rectangle with a black point in its center). Fix your eyes on the black cross without moving them for about thirty seconds. The colorful clouds will soon disappear and turn into gray nothingness.

This happens because your brain stops responding to things that don't change.* Once you move your eyes, you will immediately regain awareness of the colors. You see them again. By moving your eyes, you are changing the inputs your brain receives. Of course, it's not only constant rainbow clouds that your brain stops noticing. Over time, you stop feeling the socks on your feet or hearing the persistent buzz of an air conditioner.[12] (Perhaps you aren't noticing some background noise right now?)

You get used to much more complex circumstances too (such as wealth, poverty, power, risk, marriage, and discrimination), and this type of habituation involves active *inhibition* between different neurons.[13] For example, imagine that your neighbor, Ms. Wheeler, got a new dog, a German Shepherd named Finley. Finley barks a lot. At first the barks are surprising; you notice each one. But after a while your brain creates a "model" (that is an internal representation) of the situation ("Whenever I pass by Ms. Wheeler's house, Finley will bark").[14] You anticipate the bark. When you experience it ("Finley barks"), your brain compares the experience to the model ("Whenever I pass by Ms. Wheeler's house, Finley will bark"). If the experience matches the model, your response (neural, emotional, behavioral) is inhibited.

---

* In this case it is also possible that your photoreceptors stopped responding to the image.

With more and more experiences of Finley barking, your internal model becomes increasingly precise and will better match the actual experience of hearing Finley bark. The better the match, the more your response is inhibited. But if the match is not identical (for example, the dog sounds louder, softer, or angrier, or jumps over the fence and runs in your direction), you will be surprised, and your response will be less inhibited.

Let's try this ourselves. Look at the photo below.

If you are like most people, you were probably startled by the photo at first. You might have felt uneasy, disgusted, or even afraid for a second or two. But as long as the dog does not jump off the page and sink its sharp teeth into your smooth neck, your brain will respond less and less to its raised lips and raging eyes.[15] As a result, the uneasy feeling will eventually disappear. You have become habituated. (Something similar happens if you encounter someone with an unusual physical

appearance. At first, you will notice it and perhaps be preoccupied by it; after a while, you might be startled to see that it
barely registers.)

Your brain seems to have evolved different mechanisms,
from those involving a single cell to those involving more complex neural systems, that obey the same overarching principle.
The principle is simple: when something surprising or unexpected happens, your brain will respond strongly. But when
everything is predictable, your brain will respond less, and
sometimes not at all. Like the front page of a daily newspaper,
your brain cares about what recently changed, not about what
remained the same. This is because to survive, your brain
must prioritize what is new and different: the sudden smell
of smoke, a ravenous lion running your way, or an attractive
potential mate passing by. To make the new and unexpected
stand out, your brain filters out the old and expected.

In the chapters that follow, we will see how knowledge of
how your brain works can help you to identify ways to revel
in the good things to which you have habituated, so that phe-
nomenal features of your life may "resparkle," as well as ways
to focus on, and seek to change, the bad things you no longer
notice, including your own bad habits. We will consider health,
safety, and the environment, exploring how you can perceive
serious risks to which you have become accustomed. We will
show how becoming aware that your brain responds less to
repeated stimuli can help make you resilient in the face of repetitive misinformation from others and help you address the
chronic stress and distraction that social media triggers. We
will show how habituation and dishabituation offer lessons for

business—about what keeps employees motivated and customers engaged. We will also consider how people get used to gender and racial discrimination and even to the gradual rise of fascism, until "dishabituation entrepreneurs"—rebels who combat the norms—make them salient.

All that being said, habituation is crucial for survival: it helps us adapt quickly to our environment. When people are unable to habituate (for example, to physical pain), that inability can cause great suffering. Some people are also less likely to habituate than others. We will see how slow habituation can lead to a range of mental health problems, but also to creative insight and extraordinary innovation (in business, sports, and the arts).

We hope that what follows will help you turn off the brain's gray scale, to see colors again.

PART I

WELL-BEING

1

HAPPINESS:

ON ICE CREAM, THE MIDLIFE CRISIS, AND MONOGAMY

*If I was here for the last eighteen years doing that all
day, every day, it probably wouldn't still have pixie
dust on it. But I go away, and I miss it so much. Then
I come back, and it kind of resparkles.*

—JULIA[1]

MEET JULIA AND RACHEL. Both women are living what
many would consider charmed lives. They are in their
midfifties; Julia lives in New Mexico and Rachel in Arizona.
The two women have loving partners. Julia has three adorable
children—two sons and one daughter. Rachel has two daugh-
ters. They both have fulfilling jobs they excel at, which have
made them wealthy. They are also fit and healthy. Many people
would say they have been, well, blessed.

But here the similarities end. While in many ways both
women won life's lottery, their subjective experience is quite

different. Julia marvels at her good fortune on most days, but Rachel has become blind to her fairy-tale existence.

Julia is in awe of the miracles in her life, big and small. She says she has a "happy life." When asked about her ideal day, she says, "When there's harmony in the house and you get up and make breakfast and see everybody off to school. Then do some adventuring with my husband. We'll take a bike ride or have a coffee or a meal somewhere, and then I'll have time to myself and now it's almost three o'clock. I'll go get the kids from school. Lacrosse practice. Start making dinner."[2]

Rachel has a word for such days: "Boring!" Sure, she is aware that she has been blessed with family, wealth, health, and friends. She is not sad or depressed, but she does not experience her daily life as "happy." She says, "It's okay."

What crucial ingredient separates Julia from Rachel? It is not a personality trait or genetics. It is not the quality of their relationships with family and friends. The difference is small but significant. Julia travels for work often; she goes away for a few days, maybe weeks, and comes back home. She says, "I go away, and I miss it so much. Then I come back, and it kind of resparkles." Being away allows her to focus on "the joy of the details of life." She says: "If I was here for the last eighteen years doing that all day, every day, it probably wouldn't still have pixie dust on it."[3]

Rachel does not get to take frequent breaks from daily life, and as a result she doesn't perceive the pixie dust that covers her world. She does not get to experience life without her husband, children, and comfortable home. Instead, those things are there, in front of her, every single day. As a result, they accumulate dust and lose their sparkle.

We have a secret to share: you've probably heard of Julia before. You might have spent time with her in your living room, eating popcorn in your pajamas. Julia is Julia Roberts, the celebrated actress (and the quotations are real). We know what you are thinking: "Of course, Julia Roberts is joyful and grateful. Could there be a more privileged person?!" But in this case, we think that Julia's observations about her unusually privileged life can shed light on ordinary human experience. And we believe it may offer insight into how all of our lives can resparkle.

Now, while you have not heard of Rachel before (she is an acquaintance whose identifying details we have altered), you probably know someone who resembles her. In many ways she represents the lived reality of many people. She reflects the daily experience of many of us who might not have what Rachel has, but who do have precious things in our lives (perhaps a loving family, perhaps good friends, perhaps an interesting job, perhaps a talent) and tend not to focus much on those things, at least not from moment to moment or from day to day.

What might seem amazing to others, or what was once amazing to us, becomes part of life's furniture. We habituate to it. For example, studies show that after getting married, people report being happier on average. Yet, after about two years of this joyful honeymoon period, happiness levels tend to decline to premarriage levels.[4]

So let's try to understand why people such as Rachel stop seeing and appreciating the good things in their lives, and how Rachel can adopt a Julia perspective. Without becoming a Hollywood star with a stunning smile, that is.

ICE CREAM EVERY DAY

On a recent hike up the mountains in California, Tali and her then nine-year-old daughter, Livia, stumbled upon a gorgeous mansion on a cliff overlooking the ocean. Envision those stunning European mansions in old movies where Grace Kelly's characters find themselves. (Julia might live there now.) After gasping, Tali asked her daughter if she would like to live in such a mansion.

"No!" said Livia.

"Why not?" asked Tali.

"Well, whenever I get ice cream or a toy, it is a treat, and it makes me very happy. But if you are that rich, you get ice cream and toys all the time and so you don't appreciate it because you get it every day. It stops being a treat and you are not grateful."

Livia's point is well-taken. It is echoed by more mature thinkers. The economist Tibor Scitovsky, for example, said that pleasure results from incomplete and intermittent satisfaction of desires. This claim is worth repeating—*pleasure results from incomplete and intermittent satisfaction of desires.*[5] That means that the good things in life (whatever your fancy—amazing food, great sex, expensive cars) will trigger a burst of joy if you experience them occasionally. But once those experiences become frequent, daily perhaps, they stop producing real pleasure. Instead, they produce comfort. Scitovsky believed that wealth in particular turns thrills into nice, but boring, comfort.

We think that Scitovsky's general insight is correct, but only loosely associated with wealth. You don't need to be rich to turn intermittent pleasure into mundane comfort. Consider macaroni and cheese. Many people (including Livia) enjoy macaroni and cheese a lot, even though it may be considered a basic dish. Maybe you like this cheesy, gooey-warm pasta too. But what would happen if you ate it every single day?

We know the answer because a group of researchers conducted a controlled scientific study to find out.[6] They recruited a group of people and randomly assigned them to one of two groups. One group received a macaroni-and-cheese meal every day for a week. At the beginning of the week, the volunteers loved their meal, but gradually and with every passing day they found macaroni and cheese less and less pleasing. They simply habituated to it. Almost any stimulus that is experienced again and again close in time, whether it is a flower garden or piles of trash on the sidewalk, will evoke less of an emotional reaction, good or bad.

The other group of volunteers received a macaroni-and-cheese meal once a week for five weeks. They loved their meal on the first week. They loved their meal on the second week. They loved their meal on the third week. You see where this is going. There was no decline in how much they enjoyed macaroni and cheese, because *pleasure results from incomplete and intermittent satisfaction of desires.*

You may feel sad for the group who received macaroni and cheese every day. Please don't. Those who received macaroni and cheese every day ate less of it over time, which made it easier for them to fit into their blue jeans. Those who received macaroni and cheese every week ate the same amount every week, and some had difficulty buttoning their pants.*

RESPARKLING

Julia has "macaroni and cheese" intermittently. Once habituation kicks in, it might be time for her to jet off and have potatoes and steak. When she returns a few weeks later, "macaroni and cheese" feels divine again. Rachel, on the other hand, has been eating "macaroni and cheese" every day for decades. She can remember the excitement of the very first spoonful—the first night in her home, those first few weeks in her incredible job, the first time she kissed her spouse. But as novelty wore off, so did pleasure.

Rachel reminds us of a tragic character named Henry Francis Valentine in the old television show *The Twilight Zone*. In an episode called "A Nice Place to Visit," Henry, a criminal, is shot and killed by the police during a robbery. Waking up, Henry finds himself in the presence of his friendly guardian angel, Pip, who informs him he is dead. Henry is startled, but quickly learns that Pip is willing to give Henry whatever he

---

* While experiencing the same thing over and over will often reduce the amount of pleasure we derive from the experience, some familiarity can heighten pleasure. For example, the *mere exposure effect* is a psychological phenomenon by which people tend to develop a preference for things (art, music, faces) simply because they are familiar. So the first few repetitions may increase joy, before eventually decreasing it due to habituation.[7]

wants: money, victory at the casino, beautiful women, anything at all. "I must be in heaven," Henry thinks.

This is quite exciting at first. But after a few weeks, Henry starts to lose his mind with boredom. Apparently, money, champagne, and fast cars are not so enjoyable if you can have them constantly, any time of day. Henry cannot bear it anymore. He begs Pip to move him to "the other place"—you know, the one with burning-hot flames. "Whatever gave you the idea you were in heaven, Mr. Valentine? *This is the other place!*" says Pip.

Rachel is certainly not confusing heaven with hell. But she does not fully marvel in the joys of her own heaven on earth, because she has habituated to it. What we mean when we say "habituated to it" is that she notices the lovely things in her life (clean kitchen, works of art, green trees) less; she reacts to them less; she appreciates them less. To feel joy again she may need to dishabituate. To dishabituate to something (a certain food, a loving spouse, a great job, the warmth of sunlight, the blue of the ocean), we need to stay away from it for a while, so that its goodness surprises us again.

Even small breaks can trigger dishabituation and elicit joy. For example, would you rather listen to a piece of music from start to finish or have the listening experience disrupted with small breaks? We are guessing that you would prefer to listen to the tune with no interruptions. Most people say this when asked. But if your aim is to maximize your enjoyment, your choice may well be wrong.

In one study,[8] volunteers listened to enjoyable tunes either continuously or with small breaks and rated their enjoyment. While 99 percent of the volunteers predicted that the breaks would make their experience worse, in reality the effect was the exact opposite! People enjoyed the music more with breaks. They were also willing to spend twice as much money to hear the music in concert than those who listened with no breaks.

Breaks reduced the tendency to adapt to the good stuff, so the bursts of joy from the song lasted longer. Astonishingly, this was true regardless of what people did during the break. One group did nothing, another listened to annoying noise, and a third to another song. In all cases, breaks increased enjoyment of the original tune.

It seems, then, that most people underestimate the power of habituation and are generally unaware of the benefit of breaking up good experiences into segments. As a result, you may choose to consume good experiences (music, a massage, a movie, a vacation) all at once, instead of inducing artificial breaks that make you enjoy the experiences more (more on this in the next chapter).

Now, Rachel may not be able to jet away for breaks of a few days or weeks like Julia Roberts does, but even a night or a weekend away can trigger dishabituation. Time away, however short, will enable Rachel to perceive her life with fresh eyes—to break up her reality. But what if Rachel is unable to get away even for a weekend? Well, perhaps she can change her environment while staying in place? For example, when Tali had COVID-19 during the writing of this book (her symptoms were mild), she was exiled to the guest room in the basement of her home. She was surprised to discover that living in the basement felt a bit like an adventure. Once isolation was over and she rejoined humanity up on the ground floor, home life seemed, as Julia would put it, to have been sprinkled with pixie dust once more.

But you don't need to use your basement as an impromptu vacation destination for dishabituation to kick in—you can use your imagination. Laurie Santos (also known as "Yale's happiness professor") suggests changing your environment using just your mind.[9] Close your eyes and imagine your life, but without your home, without your job, without your family; create vivid images with color and detail. Not only is the experience horrific, but it causes most people to feel lucky about what they have.

It's a bit like having a nightmare in which you lose a loved one—when you wake up and realize it was all a dream and the person is right there beside you, you feel especially thankful. Before the nightmare you may well have *known* that you had a good thing, but after you awake from it, you *feel* it too.

Even when you have habituated to something good, you might well still *know* that it is terrific. For example, if you are lucky enough to have secured your dream job, you may no longer feel the "Wow!" when you enter your office, but you are aware that it is a great position. This is because your explicit assessment of what is good does not habituate as fast as your feelings.

In a study conducted at Haifa University in Israel, in the lab of Assaf Kron,[10] a group of volunteers were shown a series of photos of delightful things, such as an adorable puppy or a cute baby. Each photo was shown again and again—sixteen times. While the volunteers were observing the photos, their facial movements were measured using electromyography (EMG). EMG records the electrical activity produced by skeletal muscles. When you feel pleasure, the zygomaticus muscles move, which allows you to smile. These muscles extend from your cheekbones to the corners of your mouth.

When the volunteers first observed the cute photos, their zygomaticus muscles were activated quite a bit, and they reported feeling pleasure. However, over time they habituated— they reported feeling less and less pleasure with each repeated exposure to the puppy or the newborn, and their zygomaticus muscles moved less and less (a control condition showed that this was not due to fatigue). Yet the volunteers continued to rate the photos as wonderful. Although they *knew* the photos were adorable, they no longer sparked joy. What we appreciate intellectually can be dissociated from what we feel emotionally.

This separation between "feeling" and "knowing" makes sense if you consider that emotions are an old evolutionary response that human beings share with other animals low on the evolutionary ladder, while "knowing" can be seen as a much newer and in some ways more distinctly human capacity. The two rely on partially different brain systems. The "old" emotional response habituates fast, while the "new" intellectual response lingers on.

Why, though, does the emotional response habituate fast? Why have we evolved a brain that derives less and less pleasure from good things that are constant or repeated? Would it not be great if you marveled at your job/house/spouse just as you did at the very beginning?

Maybe, or maybe not. Habituation to the good drives you to move forward and progress. If you did not experience habituation, you would be satisfied with less. For example, you might end up being happy with an entry-level position many years after getting the job. Now, being satisfied with less may seem desirable, but it also means that you would have reduced motivation to learn, to develop, and to change. Without emotional habituation, our species may not have had the technological innovation and great works of art we do, because people might not have had the motivation to create them.

A delicate balance must be struck here. Habituation can lead us to be unsatisfied, bored, restless, and greedy. But without habituation (and dare we say some boredom, restlessness, and greed), we might have remained cave dwellers.

One reason why we are not all sitting in a cold and dark cave right now is that progress makes us happy. Joy often comes from perceiving yourself as moving forward, changing, learning, and evolving. Consider research conducted in London by two neuroscientists, Bastien Blain and Robb Rutledge.[11] They had volunteers report their feelings every few minutes while playing a new game. They found that the volunteers were happiest not when they gained the highest amount of money in the game (although that did make them happy too), but when they learned about the game. Learning contributed more to happiness than money. You habituate to things—a fancy car, a large-screen TV—but you don't habituate to the joy of learning because learning by definition is change. One cannot habituate to change.

In Oscar Wilde's *Importance of Being Earnest*, Ernest Worthing tells his love interest, Gwendolen Fairfax, that she is perfect. She replies, "Oh! I hope I am not that. It would leave no room for developments, and I intend to develop in many directions."[12]

Gwendolen is not alone; as Henry Valentine learned in *The Twilight Zone*, "perfect" is not a state people enjoy. In one study, Andra Geana and her colleagues at Princeton[13] asked volunteers to play a computer game in which they had all the necessary information to perform perfectly. People did not at all enjoy this game. They quickly became bored. ("This is the other place!") So Geana gave them another game to play instead. In this new game, players needed information about how to perform well—they had to learn as they went along. The volunteers were far more engaged in this new game. They had much more fun, even though they had to work hard if they aspired to perform perfectly.

Then Geana gave players the opportunity to shift from one game to the other. She found they were far more likely to shift from the game of perfect knowledge to the game of uncertainty and learning—and stay there. When we cannot learn, we get bored and unhappy.

MIDLIFE SAMENESS

When change halts—when you stop learning and progressing—depression kicks in. We believe that this is one of the core reasons for the dreaded "midlife crisis." When you hear "midlife crisis," you might well imagine a balding man in his fifties driving a red sports car. But the reality is quite different. The dip in happiness that people experience in their forties and fifties is observed in both women and men, in different countries, in individuals of different professions, and in different life circumstances—married, single, gay, straight. The dip has been found in at least seventy countries, based on surveys of thousands of people in each.[14]

The exact age at which people hit rock bottom does differ slightly across countries. For example, it is midforties in the United States, the United Kingdom, Canada, and Sweden; midfifties in India, France, Germany, and Argentina; and early sixties in Greece, Peru, and Austria. (Russia, Croatia, Poland, and Bosnia are the exceptions—there happiness reaches rock bottom only for people in their seventies or eighties.)

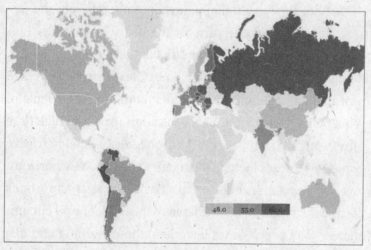

The age of greatest unhappiness around the world. The age at which happiness reaches its lowest point in countries around the world (where data was available and analyzed). The darker colors indicate "rock bottom" later in life (around sixty-two), while lighter colors indicate earlier descent (about forty-eight).[15]

Before hitting the midlife mark, many people may sense that they are learning and evolving, professionally and in other ways—learning how to be a friend, a nurse, a cook, a clerk, a teacher, a doctor, a spouse, a lawyer, an activist, a belly dancer, a pastry chef, a parent. When you are nineteen, anything might happen: you might fall in love, today or tomorrow, and you might learn something that will turn you upside down or change your life. But around midlife, many people sense that they are stuck. Their feeling is that things are stable and will remain as they are for a long time.

Stability is not a bad thing, and life may be "good" in the conventional sense. But there is less change, less learning, less that is unknown or unpredictable. People may have some great things in their life, but many of those are constants to which they have habituated.

But not to worry, unhappiness does not stick around forever. Happiness takes a turn for the better later in life. That image of the grouchy old man? The data does not support it. It may seem surprising, but happiness has been shown to rise post-midlife and continues to do so until the last couple of years of life.[16] Maybe this is because during post-midlife (late fifties, early sixties) change kicks in once again—children leave home, adventures loom, people retire and seek new horizons. It is just speculation, but perhaps the need to restructure one's life and learn how to be a different person under new circumstances jolts people from habituation into learning and dishabituation.

By contrast, midlife "sameness" can be long and demotivating. Suicide rates (especially for men) are relatively high in people's late forties.[17] The reasons for suicide are complex and diverse, but lack of change, reduced learning, and a sense of halted progress may contribute to the uptick.

REFRIGERATORS AND WATCHES VERSUS BEACHES AND CONCERTS

To fight the midlife lull, individuals may try to induce change. Peter buys a motorcycle, Jacqueline moves from one place to another, Chloe changes jobs, Muhammad learns how to garden, Viola travels to China, and Thomas takes a creative-writing course at his local college. Who will be most successful in injecting happiness back into their lives?

Well, ample research shows that experiences (vacations, restaurant meals, sporting events, concerts, courses, learning a new skill) tend to induce more joy than new possessions (cars, houses, tablets, clothing, furniture, televisions, dishwashers). You may have heard of this well-known finding before,[18] but you may not know *why* experiences (on average) make you happier than possessions.

Recall a purchase you made recently of a material good. (A new laptop? A bike? A refrigerator?) Great, now recall a purchase you made recently for an experience. (A trip to London? A meal at a steak house? Tickets to a football game?) Try to select two purchases (a material good and an experience) that cost roughly the same and that you made at approximately the same time (a few weeks or months ago). How satisfied are you with each?

If you are like most people, you are happier with the experience than the material good. Surveys show this, but we already know it, right? Here is the interesting part. When people look *back* at their purchases, they are usually happier with the vacation to South Carolina than the new sofa, the Broadway musical than the polo shirt, yet at the time of the purchases there is no difference in how happy these made people feel.[19] What's going on?

While satisfaction with material goods falls sharply over time, satisfaction with experiences does not decline. Research shows that it often increases! The joy you get from refrigerators and concerts may be roughly the same at first, but while you habituate to a KitchenAid with French doors relatively fast, the happiness that is triggered by the memory of watching Prince perform at the O2 Arena in London before his untimely death lasts a lifetime. The lingering impact of experiences on happiness relative to the fleeting impact of possessions may be one reason that people are more likely to regret not purchasing an experience (a trip to Paris, a pony ride) than not purchasing a thing.

We are not saying that all experiences are better than all possessions. Some experiences are awful, and some possessions are heavenly. As Samuel Johnson wrote, "Nothing is more hopeless than a scheme of merriment."[20]

Nonetheless, *on average* many of us seem to underrate the value of experiences and to overrate the value of material possessions.[21] One reason for this systematic error is that we think that possessions last for a long time while experiences are fleeting. It seems logical to think so—a fridge, a car, or an ornament will last for years. (Tali still wears pieces of clothing she bought when she was fifteen; that's good value for money right there.) A hike along the coast, a bungee jump, a music lesson, a stay at a fancy hotel—these things last weeks, days, hours, or minutes. But in the human mind, the possession might be ephemeral, and the experience might last forever. After a short time, you might not notice a new possession. By contrast, an experience might have lasting benefits.

Think of a spectacular diving experience, a lecture that completely changed your view of the world, a trip to Alaska. All these might return to the mind—not a little but a lot. These memories still sparkle not despite their fleetingness but *because* of it. Think of a terrific romance. Short romances may have nostalgic pixie dust scattered on top for decades, while romances that lasted for decades may be recalled with no pixie dust at all.

WHEN PARIS, FRANCE, BECOMES PARIS, IDAHO

In *Casablanca* Rick and Ilsa experience fleeting romance. When it's time to part, Rick turns to Ilsa and says, "We'll always have Paris." We are certain that Paris (and Casablanca) will be carved deep into their cortices till their dying days. But what if it were not World War II and Rick and Ilsa did not need to part? Instead, they got married, moved in together, had a couple of children, followed by a handful of grandchildren? And what if the *Titanic* never sank? What if Rose and Jack got off the grand ship together in New York City?

Oscar Wilde had a clear view on the matter: "It is very romantic to be in love. But there is nothing romantic about a definite proposal.... Then the excitement is all over. The very essence of romance is uncertainty."[22]

Not long ago, Cass was attending a wedding in New York. The conversation at his dinner table naturally turned to love and marriage. By some kind of miracle, seated directly across from Cass was an expert on the topic—the renowned couples therapist Esther Perel. Her views on the matter are not vastly different from Wilde's.

Perel has treated numerous married couples. She has observed that over the years intimacy and comfort increase between a husband and wife, or wife and wife, or husband and husband. Often love persists. But excitement, including erotic excitement, decreases.

"If intimacy grows through repetition and familiarity," Perel says, "eroticism is numbed by repetition."[23] This, then, is the paradox: greater intimacy often marches hand in hand with a reduction in sexual desire, a dimmer sparkle.

In Perel's view, eroticism "thrives on the mysterious, the novel, and the unexpected" (as Wilde had it, "uncertainty") because "desire requires ongoing elusiveness. It is less concerned with where it has already been than passionate about where it can still go." What couples forget is that "fire needs air."

Novelty and change, which are central to desire, are inconsistent with safety and predictability, which people also cherish and need. "Deprived of enigma," Perel says, "intimacy becomes cruel when it excludes any possibility of discovery. When there is nothing left to hide, there is nothing left to seek." Habit and routine are anti-aphrodisiacs. As she puts it, "Desire butts heads with habit and repetition."[24]

When you see your partner as fixed and predictable, passion is reduced or even eliminated. But that perception of predictability is only an illusion. We can guarantee that your partner has secrets, experiences, and views that you would be surprised to learn about, even if you have been together for decades. (We hope that none is of the dreadful kind, though some may be unpleasant.) The notion that you know your loved ones inside out is simply wrong, whether it is your spouse, best friend, child, or parent. Realizing that you see only a fraction of who your partner really is can keep excitement alive.

Think of a time when you were especially drawn to your partner. What was your partner doing? Where were you? When Perel asked people to describe an incident when they were most drawn to their partner, they mentioned two general situations. First, they were especially drawn to their spouse when they felt unfamiliar and unknown—for example, when they saw their partner from a distance or when they observed them deep in conversation with strangers. Second, they were especially drawn to their spouse when they were away and then when they reunited. After years of listening to couples in her clinic, Perel concludes that to avoid having Paris, France, become Paris, Idaho, less togetherness and more separateness are needed.[25]

Perel's conclusion is supported by science. A study[26] of 237 individuals showed that when people spend more time apart from their partner, they report greater sexual interest in them. Members of each couple may find their sweet spot—maybe weeks apart, weekends apart, or just evenings apart. It's a delicate balance. People need quality time together and common experiences to keep a relationship going, but some independence may be just what the doctor ordered.

If something is constant, we often assume (perhaps unconsciously) it is there to stay. We thus focus our attention and effort on the next thing on our list.[27] But if we can make the constant less so, our attention will naturally drift back to it, and if it is good at its core, it may just resparkle.

THE EXPLORER AND THE EXPLOITER

Cass's family has a phrase: "It's what we always do." The phrase is meant as a (usually) fond rebuke of Cass, who tends to like his routine. Cass's wife prefers novelty and adventures, and she's fine with a high degree of uncertainty. Cass is more of an "exploiter" of what he knows, tending to make choices with known benefits (the staycation and the familiar restaurant), while his wife is more of an "explorer" of the unknown, preferring choices with uncertain but potentially greater benefits (the vacation in an unfamiliar place and the new restaurant).

Think about your own preferences. Suppose that you are going out to dinner this Saturday night. Would you like to go to a place that you know well, and that you know you like, or instead try a new place that opened just last month? Do you enjoy meeting new people, or do you tend to think that old friends are best? Are you adventurous? When you hear the word *staycation*, do you smile or frown?

To be clear, everyone (you included) will engage in some exploitation and some exploration. We all go back to places and people that we know from past experiences are great, but also at times take risks and explore unknown avenues. But the balance between the two can vary greatly between one person and another. Some people seem drawn, by nature, to exploitation, and others to exploration.

We speculate that people who habituate quickly will be drawn to exploration. The reduction in emotion associated with habituation to some status quo will spur a search for fresh experiences and discoveries. You may call these people *sensation seekers*. Sensation seekers pursue new and different sensations, feelings, and experiences.

You know what we mean—people who travel the world, bungee jump, take psychedelic drugs, or interact with a diverse group of people. These are people who risk exploring the unknown, in part because they tend to habituate quickly to the known. But a common way for explorers to explore the unknown does not require traveling or taking psychedelic drugs. To the contrary, one can stay at home with a cup of herbal tea and some reading material.

Dani Bassett, a professor at the University of Pennsylvania, and colleagues found that explorers—those sensation seekers who like to try new things—have a specific pattern in how they seek knowledge. In one study,[28] Bassett asked 149 volunteers to search Wikipedia for twenty-one days and to record their every search. When examining the volunteers' Wikipedia activity, Bassett found that people could be neatly divided into two groups.

One group, the "busybodies," searched for information on diverse issues, creating a body of knowledge of weakly related concepts. For example, a person might read the Wikipedia page on television producer Shonda Rhimes, followed by the page on heart disease, followed by a page on artichokes. The other group, the "hunters," created tight knowledge networks by searching for information on related concepts. For example, a person might read the Wikipedia page on Barack Obama, followed by the page on Michelle Obama, followed by the page on the Obama Foundation. The type of "knowledge seeker" a person was provided clues about the person's personality—the busybodies were more likely to be sensation seekers (i.e., explorers) than the hunters.

Look at the people around you—your partner, your friends, your colleagues. Many will fit relatively neatly into the busybody/explorer or hunter/exploiter categories. Both types can be extremely interesting and successful people. Take, for example, two of the wealthiest people on the planet: Bill Gates and Warren Buffett. Both are avid readers.

Gates, the cofounder of Microsoft corporation, has been known to read a book a week since he was a child. That is approximately 2,592 books during his lifetime. His book recommendations include a book about the science of sleep (*Why We Sleep* by Matthew Walker), several about education (e.g., *Prepared* by Diane Tavenner), a book of essays on tennis

(*String Theory* by David Foster Wallace), a novel about a professor with Asperger's syndrome in search of a wife (*The Rosie Project* by Graeme Simsion), a nonfiction book about Silicon Valley's Theranos scandal (*Bad Blood* by John Carreyrou), and several history books (such as *Presidents of War* by Michael Beschloss), among others.[29] We suspect that Gates would fall into Bassett's busybody group.

Buffett is also a keen reader. He recommends reading five hundred pages a day. "That's how knowledge works," he says, "it builds up, like compound interest." What is on his list of recommendations? *The Intelligent Investor* by Benjamin Graham, *Investing Between the Lines* by L. J. Rittenhouse, *The Little Book of Common Sense Investing* by John C. Bogle.[30] We could go on, but you get the picture. Buffett's list is not a diverse collection like Gates's. It consists almost exclusively of business books, most about investment. Many are how-to books; they provide a blueprint of how to succeed in investing and business. Assuming Buffett's recommendation list reflects what he actually reads, we would guess he is a hunter.

While there is a correlation between people's tendency to seek novelty in one domain (such as travel or food) and another (such as reading material), people may nonetheless explore in some contexts, but exploit in others. Cass, for example, is a busybody knowledge seeker but a homebody exploiter.

Cass's coauthor believes that it is not an accident that Cass, who prefers a staycation over an adventure, is married to an explorer. To make the best out of life we need both—to explore the new and embrace the old. When our physiology, genetic makeup, or past experiences cause us to lean (perhaps too heavily) in one direction rather than the other, a union with a person of the opposite disposition may restore our balance. Mother nature, or human nature, may be bringing yin and yang together.

2

VARIETY:

WHY YOU SHOULD CHOP UP
THE GOOD BUT SWALLOW
THE BAD WHOLE

A change would do you good.

—SHERYL CROW

TAKE A MOMENT TO reflect on your life. Is there any aspect of it you would like to change? Perhaps you are contemplating changing your job or place of residence? Maybe you are considering embarking on a new relationship or exiting an existing one? Or maybe you are just wondering whether to take on a new hobby or to change the color of your bathroom walls? How would you know if a change would do you good?

Consider the case of a talented young professor, whom we will refer to as N. A few years ago N was hired by one of the top universities in her country. Obtaining a faculty job is quite competitive. Often hundreds of applicants vie for a position, and getting hired can be a long and elaborate process. N was thrilled to get the job. But then something unexpected happened.

Within days of starting her new position, N was having second thoughts. The new department was quite different from her old one, where she had been for many years. The faculty were different; what they talked about and cared about were different; the rules were different; the routines were different. Even the lunch options were different. N was miserable. Only weeks into her job, she considered going back to her old job.

N's is not an unusual case. Surveys show that a shockingly high number (up to 40 percent!) of employees resign within the first six months on the job.[1] These figures are different across industries but are surprisingly high in almost all sectors. More than a third of new employees leave financial-industry and health care jobs within the first year. Across all industries, the number of people who quit within the first six months is higher than the number who leave during the following six months.[2]

If you ever moved to a new place, you may well be familiar with the yearning to go back—to make a quick U-turn. Yet, within a few short months most people do adapt to a new city, new job, and new residence and in many cases end up being reluctant to leave.

Luckily, a friend suggested to N that she take a deep breath and sit back while she got used to the new department. Sure, the first few weeks can be tough as you encounter countless irritants and navigate your way through a new environment. These annoyances (maybe your office is small; maybe the administrator is strict) seem as if they will bother you forever. You crave the old and familiar. But guess what? Within a few months you will no longer notice many of the things that made you miserable on your first day.

You should let habituation do its thing before you act. Perhaps your new job, your new relationship, and your new house are not a good fit. But it is difficult to assess how happy you will be in the long run living with Wolfram in Phoenix or as the director of marketing at ChopChop before you let yourself habituate to both the bad (Phoenix is hot and dry) and the good (Wolfram makes you fresh coffee every morning).

N decided to stay. Looking back, she says she is happy she did. She had a few good years at the university. Eventually another offer came her way, and she moved to yet a third institution. Once again she experienced transition pains, which faded over time. Today N is as happy in her new position as she was in her old one. The questions, then, are: Were the moves worth it? Did a change do her good?

THE VALUE OF A VARIED LIFE

The answer to those questions depends on what you consider to be a good life. That is, what are you trying to optimize in life? We don't mean money, friendship, or power, but rather what are you hoping those things (such as money, friendship, or power) will bring you?

There are three prominent answers to this question. The first is the least surprising: in all probability, you want to be happy. Happiness is famously difficult to define, but it may mean that people want to enjoy their hours, that they want their days to be filled with comfort and joy, and that they want to avoid anxiety and pain. You may desire love, marriage, children, and a generous salary because you believe those things will bring you happiness. And sometimes they do.

N may have decided to take on a new job because she thought she would be happier. If this is the case, then perhaps the decision was not such a good one. She ended up no happier in her new job than she was in her old job (this is not surprising, as people often adapt to new situations and eventually end up at their "baseline" level of happiness).[3]

Apart from happiness, you may want to feel that your life has purpose. That is a second answer people give. Sometimes meaning and happiness go hand in hand, but sometimes they don't. If you spend an evening bingeing on a new television show, you might have a good time (if the show is good), but you are unlikely to have found the time especially meaningful. If you spend a day doing charitable work, you might find the time full of purpose, but you might not particularly enjoy it; it might be challenging or grueling.

Cass hates going to memorial services—to him, they are miserable—but he recently went to a memorial service for one of his best friends, and while Cass pretty much hated it, it was full of meaning, and he would not have missed it for the world. N's old job and her new job were similar in purpose, so seeking meaning probably played little or no role in her decision to change jobs.

Both happiness and meaning are important,[4] but things

that bring you happiness and meaning may do so less over time. You might spend seven nights in a row bingeing on a terrific television show—and by the fourth night, we predict, habituation will kick in, and the experience will be a lot less great (even if objectively speaking episode ten is as good as episode two). You might spend years in cancer research—and after a time, the sense of purpose may diminish, and wonder and gratitude might be replaced by a feeling of routine.

To be sure, there are exceptions. For example, you may feel that the pleasure and purpose you experience from raising your children have not decreased that much, or perhaps at all, over the years. Could the satisfaction that comes from doing something for others, such as raising children or charitable work, diminish less rapidly?

Imagine we gave you $5 right now to spend on yourself. You could spend it on a pair of colorful socks, a purple pen, or a chocolate bar (or two). These little presents would probably spark some joy. Now imagine that tomorrow we handed you a second $5 bill. Once more you treat yourself. On the third day we gave you $5 again, and again on the fourth and fifth days. Each day we provided the same instructions—use the fiver to treat yourself. As you would expect, the joy that you experience from a $5 gift will decrease little by little every day. To be exact, on average it will decrease by approximately one point on a seven-point happiness scale.[5] At least, this is what was found in a study in which people were given a $5 gift every day for five consecutive days.

Now imagine again that we offer you $5, but this time the instructions are to spend it on someone else. You may buy chocolate bars for your colleague, colorful socks for your spouse, or a purple pen for your daughter. The second day we again provide you with $5; same instructions. Same on day three, four, and five. Each day we ask you how happy the $5 made you. Once again, the joy the $5 induced will probably subside over time.

However, it turns out that the joy of giving habituates much more slowly than the joy of getting. On a seven-point scale, the happiness of giving subsides by only half a point over five days—that is, half a point less than the happiness of getting. Giving usually provides a greater sense of meaning than getting,[6] and this experiment suggests that the benefit from doing something meaningful for others habituates more slowly.

Okay, back to the question of what people are trying to achieve in life. Many of us try to maximize happiness; many try to maximize meaning or purpose. But you may also try to achieve another aspect of life beyond happiness and meaning—variation. You may try to live a life with new experiences, new places, new people, and new perspectives, and thus with diversity in what you see and do.

Psychologists Shigehiro Oishi and Erin Westgate call this a "psychologically rich life," and they find that a lot of people strive for such a life.[7] Human beings care about happiness and meaning, to be sure, but they also care about diversity and variety. Many say that undoing their life's biggest regret would have made their life more varied.[8]

N certainly gained variation with every move she made.

Changing jobs likely made her life more interesting and offered new learning opportunities. Those opportunities increased her knowledge and provided new ideas—all things that likely improved the quality of her work. This is why rotating employees across departments once in a while, or encouraging them to work on diverse projects, may be advantageous. In the U.S. government, people may be "detailed" from their agency or department (in, say, the Environmental Protection Agency) to another (in, say, the White House), partly because they are needed, and partly in the belief that the new experience will be enriching and improve their work when they return.

In academia, faculty members often take a sabbatical every few years—a semester in which they are relieved of their usual teaching duties and are free to work elsewhere. They may produce a book, visit other universities, work in industry for a while, or simply travel the world. That might seem like a luxury, or a boondoggle, and maybe it is. But it is not only that. Whatever they do on sabbatical, they gain variety. Variety will increase the perceived goodness of their lives and, as we will explain in chapter 5, trigger creativity.

A varied life can go hand in hand with happiness and meaning, but it's not necessarily so. You might want variety in your life even if it does not make you happier, and even if it does little or nothing to increase your sense of meaning. Oishi and Westgate found that many people would sacrifice happiness and meaning for diversity of experience, because a varied life is viewed as a good life.

NOT ENOUGH CHANGE

Change introduces variety, but it also comes at a cost; it can produce hassle and also risk, as you never know what change will bring. So people may be reluctant to make a change, even when their current circumstances are not so good or are even bad. We are not referring here to cases like that of N, who took on a new job not because she was unhappy, but because an intriguing offer came along. Rather, we are referring to people who are clearly unsatisfied—maybe with their weight, maybe with their job, maybe with their relationships—but on the fence about whether to do something about it. On average, would people who are considering changing an aspect of their life end up not only with a more "varied" life, but also with a happier one?

This is exactly the question the economist Steven Levitt sought to answer.[9] To find out if change leads to greater happiness on average, Levitt could simply have asked people how happy they were before and after making a life-altering decision and then compared their happiness to that of people who did not make a change. For example, both Lauretta* and Bernadette are thinking of leaving their marriage. Lauretta ends up leaving and Bernadette stays. Lo and behold, Lauretta is happier after leaving than Bernadette is after staying.

Well, that result may reflect the fact that Lauretta had more to gain from leaving than Bernadette, which is why Lauretta left and Bernadette didn't. Maybe Lauretta's marriage

---

* Throughout this book, descriptions of a specific study participant do not refer to an individual, but rather to a representation of a group of individuals.

was worse than Bernadette's; maybe Lauretta felt more confident about dating. A before-and-after study would not give us a proper answer. A better scientific method is needed. Fortunately, Levitt had a plan.

Levitt's plan was to randomly encourage a portion of a large group of people to make a change in their life and encourage the rest to remain in the status quo. How would he do this? With a coin toss! He invited people who were considering changing a suboptimal situation to use an online toss of a coin to inform their judgments. Heads meant change; tails meant status quo. ("Heads, I go on a diet; tails, it's all brownies and ice cream.") It seems a bit wild to think that people would use a coin toss to help make such decisions, but many of them did exactly that. Because Levitt had twenty thousand participants, and because he asked an assortment of follow-up questions, he could find out whether those who stuck with the status quo, or those who made a change, ended up happier.[10]

Amazingly, people whose virtual coin turned up heads were 25 percent more likely to make a change. More important, it turned out that change, on average, was good. Those who made a change were substantially happier than those who did not. Now, because not all participants blindly followed the coin, Levitt's study still suffered from a self-selection problem (that is, who is in the "change" and "not change" conditions is not completely random). Nevertheless, the findings can be taken to suggest that making a change (quitting or accepting a job, getting divorced or getting married) produced a big gain in happiness, and this gain was found even six months after the coin toss.[11]

To be clear, we are not recommending that you get separated from your spouse or leave your job! The people who tossed the coin were already considering a change. They were likely considering a change because they were unhappy. The finding does not mean that if you are happy in your marriage, you would be happier leaving it. Nor does the study indicate which change will be best (for example, perhaps the required change is couple counseling). Rather, it suggests that *on average* you will be happier if you alter a situation you are thinking of changing; the very fact that you are considering it implies that your current state is not ideal.

Perhaps most important, the study implies that people are not making as many changes as they should. People wrongly stick with the status quo, even when it is possible and better to try something different. In ways small and large, they keep doing the same thing—they go to the same restaurants, favor the same vacation spots, read the same kinds of books, refuse to mix it up. They neglect the good "jolt" that they can get with something new and different.

CHOP UP THE GOOD BUT SWALLOW THE BAD WHOLE

We suspect that there are two sides to this coin (no pun intended). On the one hand, you may make fewer changes than you should because you may be anxious about the unknown and underestimate your ability to adapt to new situations. On the other hand, you may be thrilled by the prospect of change, big (new home!) or small (new TV!), because you think it will bring you long-term happiness, when in fact it will bring only short-term joy before habituation kicks in.

When making changes, people think about how they will feel immediately following the change and much less about how they will feel months later. That means we both overestimate the joy of a welcome change and the horrors of an uncomfortable or scary one.

For example, when a group of students were asked to imagine being separated from their romantic partner for a few weeks, two-thirds anticipated the experience to be no less painful on weeks two, three, four, and five than on week one,[12] In other words, they failed to foresee their habituation to the pain of separation. Such a failure could have led the students to give up on psychologically enriching experiences, such as a semester studying abroad.

Forecasting habituation is important not just for life-changing experiences. Every day you make choices that may induce just a little bit more pain and just a little bit less pleasure because you overlooked the power of habituation.

As an example, imagine you had to clean a toilet. It would take about half an hour to complete the unpleasant task. Would you rather clean the toilet in one go or take little breaks every ten minutes? Or suppose that your upstairs neighbor Marvin is spring cleaning, and that you can hear the annoying noise of the vacuum loud and clear. Should you make Marvin a cup of coffee so that you both get a break from the *buzzzzzzz* of the vacuum cleaner?

Most people want the breaks. When 119 people were asked whether they would like a break from smelling a nasty odor or just have the experience over and done with in one go, 90 people said, "Breaks, please!" The vast majority—82 out of 119—also said they wanted a break from an irritating noise such as that of a vacuum cleaner. They wanted a break because they believed the experience would be less irritating with a breather.[13]

It seems like a reasonable prediction, but it is wrong. When people actually experienced the noise of the vacuum cleaner, those who were given a break suffered more overall.[14] The break interrupted the natural habituation to the unwelcome noise. The lesson is that if you need to complete an unpleasant task, such as cleaning your toilet or vacuuming your carpet, it might be wise not to chop up the experience. Once you take a breather and come back, the smell will be worse, the noise louder, and the experience grimmer overall. Avoiding breaks will facilitate habituation and so make such tasks less unpleasant.

What about enjoyable experiences? Imagine you go out for dinner at your favorite restaurant and the waiter seats you at the best table. It is nice and quiet, so you can have a pleasant conversation with your partner, and the table is also right next to a window with great views. You drink your wine and enjoy an appetizing plate of pasta. The dinner is a couple of hours long. Would you rather sit at the nice table the whole time or take little "breaks" at the back of the restaurant where it is crowded and rowdy?

"Well, that's a stupid question," you are probably thinking. Who would want to go to the back if you have a lovely spot exactly where you are? Indeed, 95 percent of people surveyed said that they would prefer not to take "breaks" from comfortable spaces.[15] But could it be, counterintuitively, that a break from a nice situation would do you good?

A nice table is pleasant, but the joy experienced during the first hour would probably fade over time. Unless . . . you break up the experience. Moving to the crowded, noisy section of the restaurant for a while (perhaps to visit the restrooms) will trigger dishabituation, causing you to appreciate the extra room and luxury offered up front. This exact experiment has not yet been conducted, so we do not know for sure if sprinkling a pleasant meal with less pleasant moments will make your experience resparkle, but evidence suggests it might. For example, customers who were given pleasant massages with breaks in between enjoyed their massage more than those who experienced the massage without interruptions.[16]

While people often prefer to keep positive experiences intact, it may be better to chop those experiences up into pieces.[17] Take vacations, for example. A few years ago Tali went on a work trip to a sunny holiday resort in the Dominican Republic. Her mission was to find out what made vacationers the happiest and why. She interviewed people about their experiences and asked them to fill out surveys. When the data was in, she noticed one word that appeared again and again and again: *first*. Vacationers spoke of the joy of "seeing the ocean for the *first* time," the "*first* swim in the pool," the "*first* sip of a holiday cocktail." Firsts seemed hugely important.[18]

As firsts usually happen earlier in a vacation rather than later, Tali wondered if people were happiest at the beginning of their vacations. Luckily, the large travel company she was working with had asked vacationers around the globe to rate their feelings throughout their holidays. Tali could use that data to test her prediction. Crunching those numbers revealed that joy peaked *forty-three hours* into a vacation.[19] At the end of day two, after people had settled in, they were the happiest. Thereafter it was all downhill.

To be clear, most people did not end up miserable at the end of the vacation. Even when they returned home, many still benefited from some warm holiday afterglow. Still, less than a week passed by before they quickly adjusted to home life— work, school runs, bills. Within seven days, it was difficult to detect any effect of the holiday on their mood at all.

This evidence suggests that *all else being equal* you may benefit the most from several small trips spread throughout the year rather than one long escape. If you take a two-week vacation, you may habituate to the wonders of the blue ocean and white sand by day three. If, however, you instead take two vacations of only four days each a few months apart, you will experience the "Wow!" of day one twice. Your overall pleasure will last longer. You will maximize firsts and afterglows, not to mention the joy of anticipating the wonderful vacation—imagining margaritas on the beach and the warmth of the sun—twice.

Of course, there are constraints to consider. Total travel time is longer if you chop up vacations into mini-ones, which may also make them more expensive. But that is not necessarily so. You may, for example, choose two mini-vacations closer to home over one faraway destination. In general, where possible you may want to chop up those pleasant experiences into smaller ones. When seated at a nice table at a restaurant, go visit the rowdy section at the back.

But when it comes to unpleasant, yet necessary, tasks and experiences, consume them all at once.

3

SOCIAL MEDIA:

HOW TO WAKE UP FROM A TECHNOLOGICALLY INDUCED COMA

We humans can adapt to a lot; it's easy to sleepwalk into a state of chronic stress and distraction without ever reflecting that things could be different.

—TIM HARFORD[1]

TWO AND A HALF years ago Sam Holstein, an author and blogger, made what she considers to be one of the best decisions of her life. Her choice was not adventurous, such as moving to Alaska, becoming a pilot, or joining the circus. No, her much more mundane decision took only five minutes to implement. But once it was done, her life changed in many ways. As she sees it, that one action made her happier, more relaxed, more productive, and more interesting, and it led to a richer social life.[2]

Sam is not alone. Many others have made the same decision and report similar effects. Take Shovan Chowdhury.

At first Shovan found it difficult to implement the change: "I could not concentrate on my studies for a few days . . . but I was determined not to go back to my previous life. I was getting used to my new life."[3] After only a few short weeks he adapted to his new life and found that he slept better, procrastinated less, exercised more, and eventually found a new job and passion.

What was the magical decision that turned Sam's and Shovan's lives around? you might well ask. Sam and Shovan decided to quit social media. They deleted their accounts on Facebook, Snapchat, Twitter, WeChat, and all the rest. But is the experience of Sam and Shovan typical? That is, would most of us benefit from quitting (or taking a break from) social media? And if so, why?

A SCALER STUCK IN YOUR MOUTH

Life has some annoying and unpleasant tasks that are nevertheless necessary to complete (going to the dentist, doing your taxes, cleaning the toilet). In the last chapter, we recommended that you "swallow those events whole," so as to allow habituation to reduce the pain. For example, if you need to have a few cavities filled, it might be better to do so in one sitting. As you habituate to the noise of the electronic dental scaler and the taste of liquid fluoride, you will suffer less than if you were to fill each cavity on a separate day.

Now imagine an alternative reality in which an electronic dental scaler was permanently attached to your mouth (we know this is impossible, but roll with us). A constant low-grade buzzing would be inside your head day in, day out, for months, maybe years. You would go to work, watch a baseball game, have a romantic dinner—all with a buzzing scaler stuck in your mouth. Because of habituation, you might hardly notice the buzz after a while. Nonetheless, the foreign object will interfere to some extent with your life enjoyment and ability to concentrate. But you might be unable to put your finger on what exactly is wrong.

Then one day your dentist decides it is finally time to remove the scaler from your mouth. The impact is unexpected. You are utterly surprised to learn how much better your life is without that buzzing piece of metal.

Just as we often fail to appreciate the good things in life until they are taken away, so we also fail to appreciate the impact of constant irritants, big and small, until they are no longer, because we get used to them. You may have experienced the ending of a not-so-great long-term relationship. At first you feel sad, but soon after you are surprised to learn how much calmer and happier you are. While you were in the relationship, you were not fully aware of how negatively it was affecting your well-being, but after it was over, the impact was crystal clear.

The only way to assess the impact of constant factors in your life that may be harming you is to take a break from them. This will allow you to dishabituate and assess those factors with fresh eyes.

Social media is a prime example of such a factor. For some of us, social media is like a constant buzzing scaler stuck in our mouth. You may suspect it is clouding your days, but you do not know if and to what extent that is so because of its constant presence.

BREAKING BAD

We would be foolish to draw broad conclusions from a handful of anecdotes such as those involving Sam and Shovan. To know whether breaking from social media is likely to improve people's life *on average*, large scientific studies are needed. Luckily, a few such studies have been conducted, and they offer some intriguing findings.

Let's say we asked you to deactivate your account on your favorite social media platform (Facebook? YouTube? Instagram? TikTok?). Would you agree to do so? No? Okay, what if we offered you cash? Still no? What if it was just for one month? How much would you ask in return for giving up scrolling, liking, and reposting for thirty days—$10, $100, $1,000? More?

This is the question economist Hunt Allcott and his coauthors asked 2,884 Facebook users.[4] They offered users money to deactivate their accounts for a month. Some people wanted thousands of dollars, which the researchers simply could not afford. But 60 percent of users said that they would be willing to deactivate their accounts for $102 or less. Allcott and his team could reasonably pay this, and they did. Their goal was to test whether a Facebook detox made people happier.

According to one estimate, people with internet access on average devote about two hours per day to social media and check-check-check their screens fifty to eighty times each day.[5] The world has more than 4.7 billion social media users.[6] So, you might think that these facts demonstrate that internet access, including use of social media, must be a wonderful thing. If people love something, where's the problem? Economists use the term *consumer surplus* to point to the gains that people get from what they consume. Because access to most of the wonders of the internet comes at a low cost, the consumer surplus would seem to be spectacularly high.

But Allcott was not sure. Yes, people choose (seemingly of free will) to go on social media for many hours. But perhaps they log on out of habit, unaware of the toll on their well-being?

To test this possibility, Allcott and his team divided those users who said they would take $102 or less to quit Facebook into two groups. The "treatment group" deactivated their accounts for a month; the "control group" did not. All the participants indicated how happy they were before, during, and after the deactivation (or no deactivation). They also indicated how satisfied they were with their life and answered other similar questions.

Before long, the data was in. Along every dimension, those who deactivated their accounts were found to enjoy their lives more. The Facebook-free group said that they were happier and more satisfied with their lives. They were less likely to be depressed and anxious. In short, no Facebook, better lives. Leaving social media behind had an effect on most people akin to its effect on Sam and Shovan. It was a bit like removing a dental scale from one's mouth. Suddenly, the constant buzz, which people did not consciously notice but was nonetheless taking a toll, was gone.

Allcott and his coauthors calculated that the increase in people's happiness from their Facebook detox was equivalent to the increase in the average person's happiness from a $30,000 rise in income.[7] That sounds like a pretty large increase.

Allcott's study is hardly the only one tying social media use to reduced happiness. Consider a study headed by the Italian Luca Braghieri, which examined the mental health data of students in universities before and after Facebook was introduced on their campuses.[8] Mark Zuckerberg launched Facebook in 2004 at Harvard. At first it was available only to users who had a harvard.edu email account. This was done partially to give the platform an air of exclusivity. For the next two years Facebook slowly rolled out across U.S. colleges. After Harvard came Columbia, next Stanford, then Yale. Slowly but surely, Facebook opened its doors to many other colleges.

Braghieri and his team used this gradual rollout to test the relationship between Facebook use and mental health. Students' mental health across U.S. universities was documented frequently with surveys, so Braghieri examined whether mental health declined in each university shortly after Facebook was launched on campus. It did. Each time Facebook made its platform available at an institution, most students created an account, and shortly thereafter the mental health of the student body declined; happiness decreased, and symptoms of depression increased. The students hit the worst were the outsiders—those who lived off campus and did not belong to a sorority or a fraternity—and those who were overweight.

Facebook became available to the rest of the public in 2008, and for the next ten years depressive episodes in the college-age population increased by a staggering 83 percent! It's difficult to establish causation, and we are skeptical of any particular number, but it is worth noting that Braghieri and his team estimate that at least a quarter of this increase is due to social media use.[9]

SHIFTING ADAPTATION LEVELS

Why are Facebook users happier without Facebook? People gained about sixty extra minutes per day on average after quitting the platform. One Facebook detoxer said, "I've been reading books and playing the piano, which I used to do daily until the phone took over."[10] People spent some of their newly freed time with friends and family (and interestingly none of it on other social media platforms). But we think there is a another, deeper reason why quitting Facebook made people happier. Social media misconfigures our perception of "normal"—it alters what we expect to experience and what we find surprising.

Consider our acquaintance Bob. Bob lives in a gorgeous house in San Francisco and has a wonderful loving wife and daughter. He is a well-known intellectual figure (we just gave him a new name and changed some identifying details), and some of you have read his books and follow him on Twitter (he has about a quarter of a million followers). Overall, Bob is satisfied with his life. However, his bliss is dampened a bit whenever he logs on to social media.

The reason? Every time he does so, he is exposed to the exciting lives of his even more famous friends. "I think to myself, 'Why was I not invited to give a talk at this fabulous conference?'" He wonders, "How come I did not get to meet the president?" His life and career, which we view as exceptional, appear a bit dim to him in the light of his über-successful colleagues.

Many of us have experienced something like that. You might log on to your favorite platform while sipping your morning coffee and learn that Fiona is currently on a sunny beach in the Bahamas, that Georgina's daughter has just been admitted to Yale, and that Patricia sold her start-up to Google for a fortune (these might be extreme cases, but you get the picture). "What am I doing with my life?" you may wonder.

In other words, your *adaptation level* shifts. This is the level of a stimulus (such as money, love, followers) to which you have habituated emotionally so that you experience it as neutral. This level is largely set by your recent experiences.[11]

Let's take income. If you earned about $130,000 a year for the last few years, you would not feel especially elated or sad when you earn $130,000 again this year—$130,000 is the level to which you had adapted. But if you receive a promotion and now earn $150,000, you will be excited for a while. Soon, however, $150,000 will become your neutral point—your adaptation level would shift from $130,000 to $150,000.

Here is the interesting bit. Although we usually assume that your adaptation level is a function of what you have directly experienced, it can also shift as a result of factors beyond your personal experience. One such factor, for instance, is your expectations.[12] Consider, for example, the following finding: prisoners report being especially frustrated just before they are set free.[13] During those last few days, they are still in their cells, but in their minds they are on the other side of the fence. This mental anticipation shifts their perception of "normal" from incarcerated to free. But in reality, they are still locked up in a small prison cell. This gap triggers such a strong negative reaction that some prisoners make the irrational decision to try to escape only weeks before their sentence is up.[14]

What we consider "bad," "great," or just "okay" depends on what we think others are getting. Studies show that whether you are happy with your sex life depends heavily on what you believe is happening in other people's bedrooms.[15] Money, outfits, relationships, real estate—how happy you are with what you have depends partially on what you believe others have.

Anyone who has two (or more) children has seen this effect in action. If, on a bright Sunday morning, you give your daughter, Daria, two blueberry pancakes with maple syrup and your son, Samuel, just one, Samuel is likely to feel aggrieved, and possibly a lot more upset than he would feel if you had given nothing at all to either. The late Antonin Scalia, a U.S. Supreme Court justice who had multiple children, once wrote:

> Parents know that children will accept quite readily all sorts of arbitrary substantive dispositions—no television in the afternoon, or no television in the evening, or even no television at all. But try to let one brother or sister watch television when the others do not, and you will feel the fury of the fundamental sense of justice unleashed. The Equal Protection Clause epitomizes justice more than any other provision of the Constitution.[16]

In this respect (and in many other respects), adults are not so different from children. We are wired to compare and contrast what we have with what others have (or what we think they have) because doing so motivates us to strive for more and to try harder. On a social level, this will lead to progress (which is good). But it can make it difficult to be happy with what we have.

Human beings have been comparing their life with that of others since the dawn of time. You can imagine your ancestors comparing the size and comfort level of their cave with that of their next-door neighbor. Yet, today compare-and-contrast has reached a whole new level. First, we do not simply compare our lives with those of the people living next door. No, today we compare our lives with those of people from all walks of life living across the globe, including the rich and famous. Second, we no longer compare our lives with the real lives of others, but we compare our lives with the highly edited lives of others.

Let's return to Bob. Without social media, Bob experiences his (privileged) life as good, even great. But after browsing through social media, his reference point changes and now his life does not seem all that wonderful. The irony is that Bob's perception of his friends' lives is unrealistic. It is based on what they choose to post, which is a biased selection of the events of their lives. Their lives are probably not nearly as amazing as they appear online. We would not be surprised if many of Bob's friends (including those who seem especially successful) do not feel as thrilled about their own existences after they view Bob's posts.

Because Bob has been logging on to social media platforms for years, he is not fully aware of the impact they are having on his well-being. He is not fully aware of how Facebook, Instagram, YouTube, and all the rest have shifted his expectations, leading to a constant feeling of mild disappointment. If Bob quit social media for a month, he might feel like one of Allcott's study participants who said, "I was way less stressed. . . . And I found I didn't really care so much about things that were happening [online] because I was more focused on my own life. . . . I felt more content. I think I was in a better mood generally. I thought I would miss seeing everyone's day-to-day activities . . . I really didn't miss it at all."[17] Without the constant tracking of others, the dust would lift, and Bob's own life might resparkle (or at least seem "good enough" rather than "not quite up to standard").

A CATCH

But there is a catch. In Allcott's study, the gain in happiness people felt did come at a cost. Those who quit Facebook were happier, but they also knew less about politics and about the news. They may have been happier in part *because* they knew less about the issues of the day. The type of information people tend to receive on Facebook—not only about news but also about family and friends—may not make them happier, but does tell them things they would like to know.

One of the Facebook quitters said he was "shut off from those [online] conversations, or just from being an observer of what people are doing or thinking. . . . I didn't like it at first at all, I felt very cut off."[18] You might want not to feel cut off, even if you end up a bit less anxious, less depressed, and more satisfied with your life.

So despite indicating they were happier without Facebook, once the month was up, and the participants in Allcott's study could reactivate their accounts, many did. People had experienced a Facebook-free life, which on average made them happier, but then went straight back onto the platform. Perhaps they wanted to learn what was going on in their country, even if what they learned made them sad, mad, and anxious. Perhaps they were concerned they would be missing out on networking opportunities and other professional prospects. Or perhaps they thought that if one lives in a society in which countless people are using a certain platform, one should continue to use that platform as well.

The choice they were making, however, was better informed. They had the experience of "breaking bad"; they could compare the benefits of a life without social media to the costs. Some decided to stay offline, while most decided to log back on.

It is not unusual to see people suffer from interactions on social media and yet stay on it. We are not just speaking of Bob's minor injuries, or of learning that some people are doing better than you are.

Not long ago one of Tali's friends, let's call her Miriam, came to Tali in tears after experiencing what Miriam perceived to be online harassment on Twitter. The ongoing harassment had a significant impact on Miriam's mental health. She could not sleep; she could not work. Her self-esteem was badly hurt. Tali suggested that Miriam log off.

With incredulity, Miriam answered, "Log off?" Her eyes widened, and she seemed alarmed. Although the platform clearly made Miriam miserable, leaving social media, even for a couple of months, was not an option in her mind. Miriam's strong urge to log on to Twitter several times a day, despite the negative consequences, looks somewhat like an addiction.

Addiction happens when a certain behavior (such as drinking, smoking, eating, exercising, posting) generates a continuous urge to engage in that behavior despite its negative effects. Part of the reason is that *not* engaging in the behavior causes pain and suffering. That is, Miriam feels anxious when she is not on Twitter. To reduce that anxiety, she logs on, only to then feel terrible when she reads nasty comments. When Miriam first joined Twitter, she did not suffer at all from not being on Twitter. That suffering emerged slowly over time the more she logged on, which created a vicious cycle. She would log on to make herself feel better, but every time she did, the suffering of not logging on increased when she was off.

If you have experienced substance abuse or lived with someone who has, you have likely seen this clearly. Benjamin Rush, a signatory to the Declaration of Independence and an early researcher on addiction, was once told by an alcoholic, "Were a keg of rum in one corner of a room and were a cannon constantly discharging balls between me and it, I could not refrain from passing before that cannon, in order to get at the rum."[19]

Some economists say that you are addicted to something

if (1) today's consumption increases tomorrow's demand (the more Miriam logs on, the more she logs on) and (2) you consume more than you wish you had (when Miriam logs off, she wishes she had spent less time on).[20] The first condition suggests a slippery slope: you begin with a little of the addictive substance (whether it is wine, cocaine, or something else), which leads to more and more and more consumption. The urge (to smoke, eat chocolate, watch TikTok videos) increases and increases. But guess what? Your enjoyment of the object of your desire does not increase.

This is partly due to habituation. On your first day on social media, you might be excited and even amazed to see that your post has gotten (say) ten likes. Wow, ten actual human beings enjoyed your words! How wonderful! But on your second day, ten likes might not have much of an impact. You might need twenty, or perhaps fifty, to get the same emotional boost that you got from ten on the first day. Because people have a weaker emotional response to a repeated stimulus, they need larger and larger quantities of that stimulus to achieve an equivalent high. That is one reason that addicts sometimes overdose.

The second condition—you consume more than you wish you had—suggests that if you help people consume less, they will. This is exactly what happens with social media—if you make it easier for people to stay away, many do.

Think about your own behavior. Would you like to spend less time on social media? In one study,[21] two thousand Instagram and Facebook users were asked to install Phone Dashboard, an app that allows people to set time limits on their screen use. They could use the app if they so desired. Desire they did. Almost 80 percent of the people used the app, and they reduced their screen time by 16 percent on average.

Once the app was installed, the users reported that they were *less likely*

- to use their phone longer than intended,
- to use their phone to distract from anxiety or to fall asleep,
- to have difficulty putting down their phone,
- to lose sleep from phone use,
- to procrastinate by using their phone, and
- to use their phone mindlessly.

Let us be clear. We are hardly suggesting that social media has only negative effects. It is a place to connect, inform, and share. People certainly gain knowledge, friendships, and jobs on these platforms. What we are saying is that for many people, such as Sam and Shovan, using certain platforms less, differently, or not at all will lead to happier and more productive lives. Many people suspect as much, and they may want to change their use to test the effects of social media on their lives. They need help to do so.

QUALITY, NOT QUANTITY

There is a large debate on whether more screen time is bad for you. We think the debate misses something important. What matters is not screen time. What matters is what you do with that time. It's not only a question of whether you spend that time on Facebook or CNN. It is a question of what type of information you are consuming. Are you scrolling through people's fake photos and curated shares, or through posts about new books or scientific discoveries?

One factor that may matter a lot is whether you are exposing yourself to negative information. Are you spending hours reading angry tweets and anxiety-inducing blogs? Tali and her colleague Chris Kelly wanted to find out if the negative information people consume online may be harmful to their well-being.[22]

They recruited a few hundred participants and asked them to go online every day for about half an hour and then send Chris their anonymized browsing history. They also completed a large battery of tests that assessed their mental health. Chris then extracted the text from the websites each person browsed and used a simple algorithm to calculate the percentage of negative words on each. He found that the greater this percentage was, the worse off people were.

You may wonder: What precedes what? Do people who have worse moods tend to seek out more negative information? Or do people who tend to find more negative information end up sad and anxious? To figure this out, Chris manipulated the information people consumed. He gave some people emotionally neutral web pages to browse and others web pages with lots of negative words, then asked all how they felt.

As you would expect, those who browsed negative web pages felt worse. He also manipulated their moods and examined the information they then chose to consume. Indeed, when Chris triggered negative feelings in people, they browsed web pages that were more negative. This means that if a large proportion of what you read is negative, it will take a toll on you mentally. But if you are in a bad mood, you will also tend to consume a lot of negative information.

When it comes to browsing, it is not as much quantity as it is quality. But it also matters who you are—are you especially sensitive to messages of anger and fear, or are you pretty resilient? Do you tend to compare yourself to others, or do you do your own thing? Different people will be affected differently.

Because of habituation, however, it is difficult to assess how "online noise" really affects your life. Noticing the impact of things that are constant is hard. We may not notice the interference caused by a TV that is on in the background until someone suddenly turns it off. Shovan said he felt "*surprised* that there is less distraction" after he altered his social media habits.[23] The only way to know is to change your usage patterns and experiment with less or different usage. You too might be surprised about what happens next.

4

RESILIENCE:

A CRUCIAL INGREDIENT FOR A
HEALTHY MIND

*Resilience is our ability to bounce back from life's
challenges and unforeseen difficulties, providing mental
protection from emotional and mental disorders.*

—MICHAEL RUTTER[1]

JOIN US IN A mental exercise. Below is a list of events. Your
task is to imagine these events happening to you. Some of
them are delightful; some are devastating; some are mildly
unpleasant. You may have experienced a few of these events
before, while others are waiting in your future, and yet others
will never happen to you.

Here we go:

1. You fall in love with the emperor or empress of a great
   nation. You get married in a lavish wedding, after which
   you join the royal household.

2. You get divorced (not from your royal partner, but from your current spouse or one in your future).

3. Your boss is unhappy with your performance and lets you go.

4. A deadly pandemic takes over the globe. You find yourself under lockdown, trapped in your home. You don't know how long the situation will last or what might happen next.

5. You take an exam and receive a grade that is significantly lower than you expected.

For each of the above events, estimate how you would feel if it happened to you: extremely bad, somewhat bad, quite good? How long do you think the event would affect you emotionally: an hour, a day, three months, ten years?

We have data on most of these events. We know how long it *typically* takes to bounce back from a bad grade, a divorce, losing a job, and a deadly pandemic. We also have a case study on becoming royalty. As you will soon discover, the numbers are surprising and interesting. But what we would like to focus on is not what is typical, but rather what is *a*typical. We will start with the mildest item on the list: receiving a not-so-good grade.

EXCESSIVE CHEWING

If you are a parent of a student, you probably know that most students care about grades quite a bit. If you yourself are a student, you probably experience joy when receiving an A and feel miserable when receiving an F (or even a D or a C). The question is—for how long? For how long would your child (or you) be affected by a grade?

Aaron Heller, a psychology professor at the University of Miami, set out to measure the impact of grades on students' moods.[2] He recruited several hundred undergraduates and (with their consent) messaged them throughout the semester to ask how they were feeling. On some days they were feeling great (perhaps they had spent the day on the beach); on other days they were a bit sad (maybe they were homesick). For each student, Aaron calculated a baseline mood (that is, how that student was feeling on average throughout the semester).

When exam time came around, the students logged on to receive their grades. Some students discovered they did well, while others found their grades were lower than they had hoped. Regardless, they immediately reported their current mood on a scale Aaron provided and continued to do so every forty-five minutes for the next eight hours.

Martin and Ronald participated in Aaron's experiment. They both received a grade of 85. Now, you probably think 85 is a good grade. Martin and Ronald did not think so. Like most of Aaron's students, Martin and Ronald were ambitious; they would have been happy with a 95 but found 85 disappointing. Martin and Ronald had different levels of baseline mood; Martin tended to be happier than Ronald. But upon receiving their grades, both reported a decline in mood of exactly half a point on a scale from one to seven relative to their baseline.

As you may have guessed, the negative effect was not long-lasting. Moments after the grade was revealed, habituation kicked in and their moods started to climb back up. But at this point Martin and Ronald diverged. Martin was back to his normal baseline mood level within three short hours. Ronald, however, took more than eight hours to recover. What differed between Martin and Ronald that enabled one to climb back to "normalcy" in less than half the time it took the other?

Martin and Ronald were the same age; they came from similar socioeconomic backgrounds; they had supporting family and friends. They planned to go to medical school and cared equally about their grades. There was, however, one important difference between the two: Ronald suffered from depression, while Martin never experienced any mental health problems.

Aaron discovered that the mood of students who suffered from depression, like Ronald, climbed back at a slower rate than the mood of healthy students, like Martin. Everyone habituated eventually, but the rate of habituation was much lengthier for students reporting symptoms of depression.* What is fascinating is that *initially* a not-so-good grade did not affect depressed Ronald more than it did healthy Martin. Rather, the effect of depression was revealed over time—depression took its toll on the ability to bounce back. The question is why.

A likely answer is rumination. Rumination is mentally "chewing" a thought over and over and over. Just as a cow brings back previously chewed food from its stomach to chew on a second

---

* Depression was not assessed as an all-or-none condition, but rather the more symptoms of depression a student reported, the longer it took them to habituate.

time, you may mentally process a negative event (like a failed relationship, an unsuccessful job interview, or a loss in a sports event) only to bring it back to mind and obsess over it yet again.

Ronald could not stop thinking about his grade. He kept worrying whether it would hurt his chances of getting into medical school. He wondered if he wasn't smart enough. Not only did he keep thoughts about the grade alive and kicking in his mind longer than Martin, Ronald also exaggerated the severity of the situation every time he thought about it. As a result, it took him longer to recover emotionally.

Rumination is typical of individuals suffering from depression.[3] Many psychologists believe it *causes* depression. That is, an inability to let go of intrusive thoughts about failure, heartache, or minor disappointments leads to depression. Martin too spent time considering why he received a not-so-great grade and what he could do better next time. But he was quicker to deploy his attention elsewhere—to his dinner plans with his girlfriend, Lauren, to the chemistry project that was due next week, to his swim team practice—and these thoughts crowded out the influence of the grade.

One of us once asked a philosopher of emotions how to stop being in love with the wrong person. Her answer: "There's only one way. Fall in love with somebody else."

FROM A WORM'S-EYE VIEW

Let us turn from minor letdowns to major setbacks. Number four on our list—a global pandemic. Remember March

2020? For us, as for so many other people, emails flooded in, announcing closures and cancelations due to the COVID-19 pandemic. Like so many others, we felt stressed and anxious. We were instructed to gather our things and leave our university offices. (Cass's assistant asked him whether this would be short-term. Cass assured her that it probably would be. Bad call.) Meetings and events we had planned to attend were canceled. The schools of our various children (two each) were closing. We gathered up plenty of canned goods (and maybe a little extra toilet paper).

We also wondered if the imposed lockdown and isolation were making people miserable. If these were significantly damaging people's mental health, then certain policies might need to be rethought. Tali and her colleagues Laura Globig and Bastien Blain decided to try to quantify the effects of this situation on the population, with the hope of informing policymakers and others of the potential harm.

It took a few weeks to put together a survey, but by late March 2020 they had data from a large representative sample of the U.S. population. Not surprisingly, the data revealed a significant increase in stress and a reduction in happiness. The changes, however, were smaller than expected. A few short months later they surveyed the same individuals again. Surprisingly, happiness levels had bounced back to pre-pandemic levels![4]

This study was not unique. Study after study revealed the incredible resilience of the human spirit.[5] The time it took people to bounce back differed somewhat from one sample to the next, but some form of habituation was observed in all samples. You flip people's world upside down, you lock them in their homes, you threaten them with sickness and death, and . . . they habituate. From *a bird's-eye view*, humans were doing all right, even amid the pandemic.

But we do not wish to take a bird's-eye view. We want to take a worm's-eye view. We don't want to focus on the mainstream, but on those left behind. How were individuals like Ronald, with preexisting mental health problems, coping?

To answer this question, we turn to British researcher Dr. Daisy Fancourt. When the pandemic first erupted in March 2020, Daisy immediately sprang into action. Like hundreds of other behavioral scientists around the world, she too put together a survey to measure people's reactions to the pandemic.[6] She wanted to know how people were feeling. Were they obeying orders? Did they agree with the government's policy? And she wanted to know whether their answers were contingent on their politics, demographics, mental health, physical health, family situation, and more.

Unlike most other researchers, Daisy managed to survey approximately seventy thousand people in the United Kingdom and continued doing so every week for the entire duration of the pandemic.[7] Years later, she was still at it. So, Daisy had the data we needed to answer our question: How well were people with mental health problems adapting to the new world?

Daisy's data was strikingly similar to Aaron's data. To illustrate, let's zoom in on two of Daisy's respondents: Shirley and Veronica. On March 23, 2020, Prime Minster Boris Johnson announced the first lockdown in the United Kingdom. He ordered citizens to fight the deadly virus by staying at home. Shirley and Veronica, both single mothers, were each struggling to cope with homeschooling, bored children, and Zoom work calls from their thousand-square-foot London flats. On Daisy's questionnaire, they indicated a decrease in life satisfaction.

When Daisy checked in with them two weeks later, both women were already doing better. The difference, however, was that while Veronica was doing only slightly better, Shirley was doing much better. What differed between Veronica and Shirley?

As you probably guessed, it was their mental health history. Veronica had been diagnosed with mental health problems long before the pandemic ever hit. Shirley had never experienced serious mental health difficulties.

Daisy's data shows that those with preexisting mental health problems were having a particularly hard time adjusting to "pandemic life." At the very beginning of the pandemic, its influence on people's life satisfaction was the same, regardless of mental health history. The greatest difference appears shortly after lockdown commenced. People like Shirley who were never diagnosed with a mental health condition reported a huge climb in their life satisfaction only two weeks (!) after the prime minster first declared a national emergency. By contrast, people like Veronica who suffered from mental health problems experienced only a slight improvement at first.

We do not know for sure why and how Shirley's happiness climbed so much in just two weeks, but we can make an informed guess. First, Shirley likely changed her environment to make it more "pandemic friendly." Perhaps she rearranged her home to make it more comfortable for herself and her kids. Tali and her colleagues found that most people reported that their living conditions had improved following the pandemic because they made adaptive changes to their physical environment. Shirley may have figured out a new schedule that worked for her and likely learned how to operate Zoom, Google Classroom, and other tools needed to work and learn from home. Maybe she came up with entertaining homebound activities to engage her family. (Fun fact: searches for "how to make banana bread" and "how to make a cocktail" spiked during the pandemic.) Perhaps her mind was no longer occupied with playing worst-case scenarios.

These types of adaptive reactions were not unusual for Shirley. She reacted similarly after her divorce and when she was laid off from a previous job a few years earlier. On average, it takes two years to adapt to big life changes such as divorce, after which people often reach their baseline level of happiness once again.[8]

As for Veronica, she eventually made some changes to adapt to government restrictions, but she did so slowly and, as a result, suffered for longer. She did not experience a significant improvement in happiness until June 2020, when schools and shops finally reopened and the sun came out from behind the gray clouds.

We don't know why Veronica experienced mental health problems to begin with, but again we can hazard a guess. Studies generally point to a combination of nature and nurture.[9] That is, certain people have a genetic sensitivity to stressors (such as a pandemic, divorce, a not-so-good grade). When they experience adversity (such as the loss of a loved one), it triggers a strong reaction, leading to a range of symptoms.

One of the ways to support Veronica, and others like her, during turbulent times is to offer them a larger piece of the resource cake. During the pandemic, governments around the world helped citizens with stimulus payments, tax benefits, and childcare. Different factors, such as income and marital status, were considered when deciding how to allocate such resources. In the United Kingdom, for example, schools were open during lockdown to serve the children of essential workers.

Daisy's data, and data from other studies like hers, suggests that one critical factor to consider when allocating resources is mental health history, because people with mental health challenges struggle to habituate and adapt.

THE EMPRESS AND POST-PANDEMIC ANXIETY

As the COVID-19 pandemic was slowing down, many people were baffled to discover that they did not feel joy. Instead, they felt anxious. The sentiment was so widespread that psychiatrists coined a new term to describe it: *post-pandemic anxiety*, understood as the angst experienced by the prospect of resuming "normal life."[10] People who previously could not imagine spending so much time at home, in part because they had habituated to working in an office, now could barely imagine working in an office, in part because they had habituated to working at home.

During the pandemic, we all got used to spending our

waking hours within the same four walls and interacting with a handful of individuals at most. Commuting, parties, travel, and dinner at restaurants were all a thing of the past. Activities that seemed effortless before, such as getting up every morning and changing out of our comfy sweatpants into a dark blue suit, would now induce stress. Events that we used to look forward to with great anticipation, such as a vacation or a concert, suddenly seemed overwhelming. We had spent months habituating to "pandemic living," as well as adapting our routines and expectations. Consequently, the prospect of changing once again filled people with dread. Change is hard because it makes us feel as if we are losing control. This is also true when changes are seemingly desirable.

Consider the story of the Japanese empress Masako.[11] In 1986 Masako Owada, a twenty-three-year-old law student, attended a tea party in honor of the Duchess of Lugo from Spain. That gathering changed her life forever. One of the other attendees was Prince Naruhito of Japan. As the true-life fairy tale goes, the prince was instantly smitten with the bright Masako and a courtship began. Eventually they tied the knot.

Obviously, when a person marries into royalty, life is completely overhauled, and this was certainly the case for Masako. Before moving to Tokyo to take up law, she attended high school and then college in Massachusetts. She found it extremely difficult to adjust from modern living in the United States to the ancient traditions of the royal household. Being in the public eye was a further stressful adjustment.

Some people in Masako's situation would eventually habituate, but Masako did not. Ultimately, she was diagnosed with a condition known as adjustment disorder. Approximately 12 percent of people will suffer from this condition, in which individuals experience sadness, hopelessness, and a feeling of being overwhelmed in response to major life changes, bad or good.[12] Ironically, positive events such as obtaining a new dream job, recovering from cancer after a long struggle, and finding love can all trigger an episode. Despite being part of the royal family for decades, the empress never recovered.

While a failure to habituate is the defining feature of adjustment disorder, it seems to characterize nearly all mental health problems. This failure has different masks, generating a variety of symptoms, but the basic problem is shared across mental health conditions.

ONE BIRD AT A TIME

We have seen that individuals with mental health conditions, such as Ronald, Veronica, and Empress Masako, have a particularly rough time adapting to life changes, good and bad (such as a global pandemic or a royal marriage) and to salient life events (such as a bad grade). But emotional habituation to positive and negative events is not the only thing that breaks down in mental health conditions; other forms of habituation fail too.

Consider the following example. As you probably remember from earlier chapters, when your brain perceives a constant stimulus, it will respond to it less and less over time. In general, this is a good thing because by ignoring things that do not change, resources are freed up to focus on potentially consequential events.

Consider faces. When you observe a frightened face, your brain reacts. Faces in general, and those conveying emotional expressions in particular, are salient. They often contain important information: Is the person angry or happy? Sad or uninterested? The face might raise questions that need answering: Why is the person afraid? Perhaps I too am in danger?

So it makes sense that your brain will respond strongly, signaling that the thing in front of you is important. If the same face appears again a few seconds later, neural activity will be reduced, and next time even more so.[13] This is because once information has been processed, there is no reason to react. But such habituation is absent in people with schizophrenia. They will observe the same emotional face again and again and again, and each time their brain will respond as strongly as it did before.[14] It is as if their brain is processing the information anew every time.

It is not just faces. A similar phenomenon is observed in response to a range of other stimuli.[15] People with schizophrenia also find it difficult to ignore constant sounds, such as a street racket or office noise. Unlike with most people, neurons in their auditory cortex fail to decrease their response over time to repeated auditory stimuli such as chatter or sirens, which can make concentration difficult.

All this shows the critical role of habituation for good mental function. We don't stop to think about this important feature of the neurons in our brain, but once this ability is impaired, a range of problems emerge, ranging from depression and schizophrenia to phobias.

Our colleague Lina, for example, is afraid of birds. Pigeons, bluebirds, hummingbirds—she is terrified of them all. When the small creatures zoom in her direction, she screams and runs away. Bird phobia is her only quirk, but it is problematic. She suspects that Hitchcock's classic film *The Birds* is the cause. Visions of violent birds attacking Tippi Hedren and Rod Taylor have been permanently stamped in her mind from a young age.

While bird phobia is relatively rare, it is common enough to have a name: ornithophobia. Apparently, Lina is in the company of many well-known and talented people reported to suffer from ornithophobia, including Lucille Ball, Ingmar Bergman, Scarlett Johansson, and David Beckham.[16] Like all mental health problems, phobias are resistant to fame and fortune.

Lina does what most people with a phobia do—she tries her best to avoid the source of the terror. She lives in London, but stays away from Trafalgar Square, where you can find hundreds of pigeons in pursuit of seeds. She has never handled a bird nor watched that terrifying Hitchcock classic again.

Here is the problem. Because Lina avoids encountering birds up close, she has little opportunity to habituate. To habituate you need to encounter the source of your fear again and again, whether it is birds, heights, spiders, or public speaking. As long as nothing disastrous happens (such as a bird pecking your eye out or tomatoes being thrown at you onstage), your fear subsides over time and you experience less stress when you think about, or indeed encounter, the object of terror.

The catch is that individuals with phobias will go out of their way to avoid the source of the fear. (People with depression adopt the same strategy. They tend to avoid situations that may lead to disappointment or trigger anxiety, such as initiating social interactions or applying for a job.) Often this interferes with their daily functioning. This is where exposure therapy comes in.[17] Exposure therapy is the most common therapy for phobias and obsessive-compulsive disorder (which often involves germophobia). The goal of the therapy is to expose you to the very thing that terrifies you in order to achieve habituation. The key is to control the exposure such that it is gradual—one bird at a time—and to do so in an environment that feels safe.

For Lina this might mean first watching videos of birds repeatedly until that no longer produces strong fear. Next, Lina might try to be in the same room with a caged bird. Once she masters that challenge, she might try to be near a bird that is held by another person. And so on and so on. One small step at a time until she finally feels comfortable touching a bird.

In Lina's case, restoring habituation is essential for overcoming a phobia. In Ronald's case, restoring habituation is essential for overcoming depression. The general principle is true for many people with problems similar to those of Lina and Ronald: a failure to habituate swiftly to people, sounds, and things can leave people feeling scared and helpless. Yet, as we are about to see, while failure to habituate can lead to mental health problems in some people, it can lead to creativity and astonishingly innovative thinking in others.

PART II

THINKING AND BELIEVING

5

CREATIVITY:

OVERCOMING THE HABITUATION OF THOUGHT

Without change there is no innovation, creativity, or incentive for improvement.

—C. WILLIAM POLLARD[1]

S A TEENAGER, DICK Fosbury felt like a flop. A student at Medford High School in Oregon, he loved sports, but he was not especially good at them. In high school he aspired to join the football team, but was told he was too small. So he tried the basketball team, but was told he was unskilled. So he joined the track-and-field team, but there too he struggled to find his place. He finally settled on the high jump, but failed to clear five feet—the minimum required to qualify for many high school track meets. Fosbury knew he had to make a change if he was to, in his own words, "first of all, stop losing, and second of all, stay on the team."[2]

If you watch a high jump event today, you will see the

athletes run toward the bar following a J-shaped route, then jump over facing the sky with their back to the bar. This technique, the Fosbury flop, is named after its inventor—Dick Fosbury. But in the early 1960s, when Fosbury was still in high school, all the athletes jumped facing forward.[3] That was how it was done, and no one thought of doing it differently. Until Fosbury came along.

People laughed at him. They thought that the Fosbury flop was absurd. They thought he was going to break his neck. "I don't think many people took him too seriously," said Frank Toews, a teammate.[4] No one jumped like that.

But Fosbury had the last laugh. In 1968 he won the gold medal in the high jump at the Olympics. As one of his college friends put it, "Everyone was talking about revolution, but there was this herd mentality of copycats; one guy grew his hair long, so everybody else did. But he had something truly different. Dick Fosbury was the only true revolutionary I ever met."[5]

When you observe people doing the same thing in the same way, over and over, your mind stops registering their action; it stops responding. In a sense, you habituate. You expect people to sit at the front when they drive and the back when they don't; to wear shoes on their feet and gloves on their hands; to eat ice cream with a spoon, not a fork. So when people do any of those things, there is nothing much to process. There is no "surprise" signal in your brain to draw attention and make you think, "Hey, maybe we can do things differently?"

But once in a while someone does come along and wonder whether the way we have always done things is the only way, the best way. Someone who thinks, "Hey, maybe humans can travel by air, not only on the ground?" or "Hey, maybe books can be sold online rather than in a physical store?" or "Hey, maybe you can jump higher facing backward rather than forward?" The question, then, is: What makes certain individuals dishabituate to the status quo and ultimately innovate?

Part of the answer is need. If Fosbury excelled at forward-facing high jumps, he would probably not have given the technique a second thought. But Fosbury could not make the standard jump work for him. His frustration, which luckily was combined with a dose of ambition, was key in nudging him to think about whether and how he could jump differently from the rest. In some sense, Fosbury's flops led to the Fosbury flop. But need is just the beginning, and it is hardly enough.

The early 1960s were already a time of change in high-jumping, even before Fosbury came up with his revolutionary backward jump. First, while all athletes were jumping forward, they were using two different techniques: the straddle method and the scissors method. The two are quite different from each other.[6] This variety in the field signaled that more than one solution was possible. Second, the high jumpers' physical environment was changing. The existing sawdust, sand, and wood-chip landing surfaces were being replaced with three feet of soft foam rubber. The new and softer surface opened up the possibility of landing on one's back without injury.

Fosbury needed that. But beyond this practical aspect, the change of surface may, in and of itself, have encouraged Fosbury to think differently about jumping.

PRIMED FOR CHANGE

How might a small change, such as a new landing mattress, boost innovative thinking? Experiments suggest that even minor changes have the power to trigger dishabituation by signaling that a new situation needs to be navigated. As a result, people are more likely to rethink the status quo. For example, after people move to a new country, they become better at solving creative puzzles.[7] Presumably, the need to deal with a completely new environment increases flexible thinking. This mental transformation generalizes to all aspects of life, including puzzle solving.

But you don't need to uproot to another country to enjoy a creative boost. Modest changes, such as going for a run after sitting at your computer for a while, help too. A large body of literature links physical activity to creative thinking.*[8] Most people assume that physical exercise increases creativity because it improves mood, but that's not the whole story.

A series of experiments led by Kelly Main[9] revealed that change in activity in and of itself (for example, from sitting to walking *or* from walking to sitting) enhances creative thought because it gears the mind for change. To measure creative thought, Kelly asked volunteers to complete one of two tasks. In one task, volunteers were given groups of three words and asked to find a fourth word that could be attached to each of the other words to create a compound phrase. For

---

* Note that while a meta-analysis of the relevant literature suggests the relationship between the two exists, the effect size is small.

instance, if we gave you the words *cup, fingers,* and *peanut,* you could respond with . . . *butter* (*buttercup, butterfingers, peanut butter*).

Here are some more examples for you to try:

1. sense, courtesy, place
2. political, surprise, line
3. dream, break, light
4. flake, mobile, cone
5. river, note, account*

People who do well on this task tend to score higher on other measures of creativity too. But Kelly and her team did not rely only on this task to measure creativity. They also asked volunteers to come up with unusual uses for household items. For example, try to think of uncommon uses for an empty paper-towel roll. Maybe you can insert rolls into your boots to keep their shape while in storage, or maybe you can use them to store rubber bands in. People who come up with many unusual uses tend to score higher on other creative tasks as well.

The key to Kelly's experiment was that one group of volunteers was seated while completing the tasks, while another changed from seated to walking and then back again to seated. Kelly found that the group that was always seated came up with fewer unusual uses of items and fewer

---

* If you are curious about the common answers to the above word triplets, they are 1. common; 2. party; 3. day; 4. snow; 5. bank.

compound-word answers. She replicated this result three times with different groups of volunteers. Even more interestingly, she found that the boost in creativity was most prominent both shortly after people started walking *and* shortly after they sat down. This suggests that *change* per se may increase creative thought.[10]

Revealingly, the boost in creativity subsided over time as volunteers habituated to their condition. That is, walking boosted creativity at first, but as people continued walking, they got used to it, and creativity subsided. On average, the boost in creative thought lasted for about six minutes after people started walking. Once people sat down, creative thinking went up again, only to subside after habituation (this time to sitting) kicked in.[11]

That was not all. Merely anticipating change was enough to boost creative thought. When the scientists told the volunteers that they would shortly change their activity, the researchers observed an increase in creativity scores. Kelly and her team believe that this is because when people anticipate change, their mind gears up for the need to process information differently, which leads to more flexible thought.[12]

Mind you, the effects Kelly and her team found were relatively small. Yet, even a small boost in creativity may help us move closer to that elusive eureka moment. So it may be a good idea to get out of your chair and have a little walk or go for a jog. Or perhaps change your work environment occasionally. Move from your office to your kitchen to a coffee shop, then go back again. Such variations may work too.

THE VALUE OF SLOW HABITUATION

Okay, so Kelly's work suggests that change increases creative thinking and habituation reduces it. Does it then follow that people who habituate more slowly are more creative? The psychologist Shelley Carson, who has written extensively about creativity, suspected so.[13] Slow habituation may enable a person to see what others no longer do and therefore perceive opportunities for improvement.

Most people are quick at creating expectations of what will happen next, when, why, and how. They are quick at generating a mental model of the world around them. But if you make fewer assumptions of how things should be, you may be open to new possibilities. Different variations of this idea had been floated by scientists before but had not been properly tested. Shelley and her colleagues decided to do so.

Shelley's first step was to identify a group of "eminent creative achievers," as she called them. These are individuals who have made a significant contribution to a creative field—for example, people who had an invention patented or a book published or had a private showing of their artwork or sold a musical composition or won a national prize for scientific discovery or other such achievements. She would compare these eminent creative achievers to those who did not qualify as such.

Next, Shelley gave both groups a task that measures how fast they habituate. To describe the task, consider the following scenario: Imagine you take our advice and go for a run. You enjoy listening to music while you jog, so you put on your headphones and play a "get up and move" song list. To monitor your speed and distance, you use a running app.

Every five minutes the volume of the music turns down a notch and a monotonous voice says something like "Distance: 4.6 miles; average pace: nine minutes and thirty-two seconds per mile." This happens again and again and again. The reported distance changes every five minutes, and the average speed may change too, but the voice is the same, the tone is the same, the structure of the sentence—the same. Because of this repetitiveness, many people will stop paying attention to the information. Their brain filters the highly predictable voice and fails to register the exact distance and pace.

Shelley didn't ask people to use a running app, but the task she used was similar in principle to the scenario above.

First, she played volunteers the same sounds again and again. Because of habituation, after a few repetitions most people stopped processing the sound, just as they are likely to stop registering the utterance generated by their running app. Next, Shelly introduced a twist. To describe the twist, imagine that while you are jogging, you meet your friend Joleen. Joleen is also out on a run, and you decide to jog together.

Joleen does not have a running app, so you promise to share with her the average speed every five minutes. But your brain keeps filtering out the app voice, so you fail to report the speed to Joleen. If you are a "fast habituater," you will do worse; if you are a "slow habituater," you will do better.

The twist Shelley introduced was similar in principle. She presented the volunteers with the sounds alongside simple images (such as a yellow circle) and examined if they learned associations between the sounds and the images. That is, the volunteers had to figure out which sound was paired with which image and in which order. Shelley had some volunteers (a mix of "creatives" and "noncreatives") complete the association problem without being preexposed to the sounds, while others (a mix of creatives and noncreatives) did the habituation task first. By comparing the performance of the creatives who were preexposed to the sounds with the performance of the creatives who were not preexposed, Shelley could measure the impact of habituation on the creative group. She did the same for the noncreatives.

She found that the creatives were less affected by repetition than noncreatives. That is, despite hearing the same sound over and over, creatives still attended to, and noticed, the sounds well enough to complete the association task.[14]

Does that mean creatives habituate slower? Or maybe they *dis*habituate faster when needed? Or maybe both? Shelley's study cannot answer these questions directly. But other scientists have examined physiological habituation directly, and they found that more creative people do indeed show less physiological habituation (as measured by skin conductance response) to sounds.[15] It seems, then, that a *failure* to habituate may indeed be related to innovative thinking.

In the previous chapter, we discussed studies that found a failure to habituate in people with mental health problems. People suffering from schizophrenia, for example, also show slow habituation to sounds. Shelley believes that what may seem like a deficit in some people may end up being an advantage in others. Inability to filter out seemingly irrelevant information can lead to difficulties of various kinds (such as an inability to focus). But it may also provide the mind with a large range of information to play around with and recombine into unusual and original ideas. Shelley thinks the latter is especially true in people with a high IQ.[16] Provide an intelligent mind with a random mix of seemingly irrelevant information, and once in while a brilliant new idea will emerge.

OUT OF A RUT

We don't know if Fosbury was a slow habituater, but we do know that he had access to an unusual mix of information that was critical for his innovation. A key to Fosbury's success was that in addition to being an athlete, he was an engineering student. His knowledge of mechanics enabled him to perfect the backward jump.

Fosbury developed his unusual jump slowly over two years, combining engineering theory with physical practice. First, Fosbury discovered that by arching his back, his center of gravity would stay below the bar as his body cruised over it. Second, he completely changed how he approached the bar. Instead of sprinting forward like everyone else, he sprinted diagonally. And while the other jumpers took off at the same spot regardless of the bar's height, Fosbury moved his spot farther away from the bar as it was raised. This trick increased his "flight time" and was critical for his success.

It was a huge departure from normal; most jumpers took

off about one foot away from the bar, but Fosbury would take off as far as four feet away to attempt the very high bars. Many coaches thought that Fosbury was crazy. One of his high school coaches told another, "He's never going to be a jumper unless he gives up this god-awful whatever you call it. If we teach him to straddle, maybe he can score for us at district. But with this—not gonna happen."[17]

New thinking, and real originality, often comes from people who are in some sense outsiders—individuals who have different knowledge or skill sets from others in the field. In law, some of the most creative work in the last fifty years has come from the field of economics. Lawyers with economics training, and economists interested in law, have asked, "If we look at the law from an economic perspective, how might we think differently?" It isn't exactly the Fosbury flop, but it produced a Nobel Prize for Ronald Coase in 1991.

In economics, some of the most creative work in the last fifty years has come from the field of psychology. Economists with an interest in psychology, and psychologists interested in economics, have asked, "If we look at economic questions from a psychological perspective, what would we do differently?" That question produced Nobel Prizes for Daniel Kahneman, a psychologist, in 2002; for Robert Shiller in 2013; and for Richard Thaler in 2017.

Thaler, probably the most pioneering of behavioral economists, might well be seen as the Dick Fosbury of the social sciences. He wasn't especially good at math, so his academic promise was not exactly terrific; in his own words, "I was only an average economist with rather modest prospects." At the age of thirty-two, he says, "I decided, come what may, I was going to pursue the possibility of combining psychology with economics"[18]—which put him in a position to invent something new. In many areas, the Fosburys and Thalers among us inject ideas from unexpected places into domains where things have gotten stuck—domains where people are in a rut.

We have all been there—our minds do the same old thing, day in, day out. It is true of poets, novelists, artists, biologists, engineers, architects, and musicians. It is true of historians and screenwriters. It is true of athletes, and it is true of people in business and government.

Cass can report that bureaucrats often find themselves in a rut. Public servants who have worked in the same job, day after day and year after year, tend to be terrific at what they do, and highly professional, but they sometimes find it difficult to imagine doing things differently. Because they are habituated to certain ways of operating, they take long-standing patterns and practices for granted. This is due not only to risk aversion, but also to a failure even to consider what risks one might take.

The same often happens in industry. Highly successful companies get in a rut by continuing on the same path they have been traveling for a while. In such cases dishabituation is often triggered by newcomers, who inject new ideas into organizations not because they are smarter or more creative by nature, but because they have not yet settled into the usual patterns. Instead of doing what has always been done, they look at things sideways or from a distance, or from very different starting points.

But flexible thinking need not emerge solely from newcomers. Organizations can increase creative thought by inducing small changes to routines and environments, just as Kelly Main and her colleagues did. For example, they may change employees' physical surroundings, encourage employees to train in fields very different from their own, create diverse teams with different kinds of expertise, or ask employees to rotate through different kinds of jobs. As a result, some may end up jumping differently.

The problem is that sometimes the rest of the field is not ready for the innovation. Most high jumpers were at first skeptical of Fosbury's backward jump and tried to persuade him to align himself with the norm. But all that changed during the U.S. trials for the 1968 Olympics. Using his unusual technique, Fosbury did relatively well, but he was still only in fourth place as the bar was raised to 2.2 meters. He had to place at least third to make the team. Ed Caruthers, one of Fosbury's competitors, cleared the bar on his first try. Then Reynaldo Brown did the same. But John Hartfield, who was leading the competition until that point, failed all three of his attempts. All Fosbury had to do to get to the 1968 Olympics in Mexico City was to clear that bar, and he did.[19]

The rest is history. Fosbury competed in the 1968 Olympics in the high jump. He did not just win the gold medal; he set the Olympic record, with a jump of seven feet, four inches. He did so not just by jumping better, but by jumping differently. Once Fosbury proved to the world the superiority of his technique, the field followed. By the next Olympics in 1972, twenty-eight of the forty jumpers used the Fosbury flop.[20]

With that, Fosbury essentially lost his advantage. The secret of his success was not his muscles or speed. It was his mind. But once his innovation was known to all, those with better physical abilities took his place on the podium. Fosbury never made it to a second Olympics, but his invention certainly did. Today, seeing athletes jump backward is the norm—something to which fans of the sport have all habituated.

In 1988, two decades after Fosbury won Olympic gold, a high school coach, just for fun, demonstrated the straddle method, which had dominated the sport for so long. One of his jumpers responded, "What in the world is that?" Another exclaimed, "Now *that* is goofy!"[21]

In high-jumping as well as elsewhere, the intriguing question now is: What will be the next big flop?

6

LYING:

HOW TO KEEP YOUR CHILD FROM GROWING A LONG NOSE

*It starts out with you taking a little bit, maybe
a few hundred, a few thousand. You get
comfortable with that, and before you know it,
it snowballs into something big.*

—BERNARD MADOFF[1]

TALI HAS A SON named Leo. When Leo was three weeks old, Tali took him to the emergency room. "He hardly cries and he sleeps through the night!" she explained to the bewildered doctor, who did not seem at all alarmed. "Babies are not supposed to be so calm," she tried. "His sister used to scream all night."

The kind doctor had other crises to manage, but to put Tali at ease, the doctor examined Leo. First, she took his temperature and listened to his heart—all normal. Next, she tested his pupils—they were the perfect size and shape. She checked his hearing and Moro reflex—all intact.

"He is a happy baby and a good sleeper," she concluded. "Count your blessings."

Tali did just that.

Six years later Leo still goes to bed happily every night—just as long as his older sister, Livia, does too. He can't bear the thought of her having fun while he is asleep. She, on the other hand, does not need as much sleep. What to do?

One option would be to tell Livia to pretend she is going to bed, then allow her to get up once her brother falls asleep. But could a small lie, repeated night after night, make Livia comfortable with fibbing? Would Tali unintentionally be triggering a deep psychological process that would increase, ever so slightly, Livia's chances of becoming the next Elizabeth Holmes? If Tali intends on raising an honest child, should she be concerned about seemingly harmless small untruths?[2]

To answer this question, consider one of Tali's childhood friends, Jonah. Jonah was a talented, smart, well-liked, and self-assured kid. He had, however, one unusual feature he was insecure about: he was born without his right pinkie toe. Jonah was concerned that the other kids would mock him for having nine toes instead of ten, so he kept his anomaly a secret.

This was not easy. In the heart of the Negev desert, where Tali grew up, sandals were worn 250 days a year, and from April to October the most popular after-school hangout was the community pool. Jonah had to constantly make up excuses for why he was keeping his shoes on. "I can't jump into the pool today because of the sniffles," he would say. "My cat ate my flip-flops," he claimed.

Lies became second nature to Jonah. Over time, he told

more and more of them in situations that had nothing to do with his right pinkie toe. If he could think up an excuse that would get him out of an inconvenient task, he did. When a polished version of the truth cast him in a better light, he adopted it. Most of us lie occasionally. But for Jonah small lies became an unconscious habit.

THE BRAIN HABITUATES TO DISHONESTY

Is Jonah particularly immoral or flawed? Perhaps. Or maybe he is just an average joe who found himself in a unique situation, mistakenly believing that the only way to avoid humiliation was to lie. One lie led to the next, which led to another. Tali suspected that Jonah was not much different from the rest of us. If any of us found ourselves in such circumstances, would we slide down the slippery slope? To find out, she and her colleagues put one hundred honest citizens at the top of a slippery hill and gave them a small shove.

They invited those one hundred people to participate in pairs in a study that was conducted in Tali's lab in central London.[3] One of these pairs were Leanora and Rina. Upon arrival the women were greeted by Neil, the lead researcher. He explained that during the experiment they would observe a series of jars partially filled with coins. Their task was to guess how much money was in each jar. Leanora was to complete the task in a brain-imaging scanner, while Rina was to complete the task in an adjacent room.

There was a small twist: Leanora would be shown large

images of the jars on her screen, while Rina would be shown small, fuzzy images on hers. Leanora would thus need to advise Rina on how much money was in each jar by communicating via Wi-Fi. Rina would then convey her guess to Neil, and the more accurate she was, the more money Rina and Leanora both would receive.

Neil left Rina in the testing room and took Leanora down to the MRI scanner and told her of yet another twist. "Rina does not know this," he whispered, "but while she will be paid the most if she guesses the correct amount in the jar, you—Leanora—will be paid the most if Rina *over*estimates the amount of money in the jar."

Neil did not instruct Leanora to lie, but in this situation lying would benefit her financially at the expense of Rina. Leanora now had a conflict of interest: her task was to advise Rina to the best of her ability, but Leanora would earn more money if she lied to Rina. The situation is like that of a real estate agent representing a buyer. The agent's task is to get the buyer the best deal possible. Yet the more the client pays for the home, the more money the agent will pocket (as agents receive a percentage of the sale price).

What did Leanora do?

Like most volunteers in our study, she started off by lying, but by only small amounts—a few pence here and there. But as the experiment progressed, she lied by greater and greater amounts. By the end of the study, she was hugely overestimating the number of coins in the glass jars. We wondered if Leanora was in fact lying or was innocently misestimating the number of coins in the jar. So, on some trials we told her she would receive the most money if Rina was accurate in her estimates. Lo and behold, when Leanora was incentivized to give Rina truthful advice, Leanora did. She could estimate the number of coins in a jar perfectly well. She simply chose not to do so when it was not advantageous for her.

While Leanora was performing the task, we recorded her brain activity. At first, parts of her brain that signal emotion, such as the small almond-shaped region deep in the brain called the amygdala, responded strongly when she lied. Why would her amygdala be active? Well, like most people, Leanora believed that lying was wrong,[4] and so every time she lied, she experienced a negative feeling.* The amygdala response was affected by the magnitude of her lie, and this response was detected only in her emotion network, not in other brain areas.

Here is the most interesting thing. With each additional lie she told, we observed a reduction in her amygdala's response—a form of habituation to her lying. The greater the drop in her brain's sensitivity to her dishonesty, the more she lied the next time she had a chance. In the absence of that uneasy feeling people usually experience when they act immorally, there was nothing to curb her dishonesty.

Leanora's behavior was typical. Examining our volunteers' data, we found a general effect: as the response in the brain's emotional system to lying decreased, the amount by which

---

* This negative feeling, which keeps us from lying, may be evolutionarily advantageous. This is because while lying can lead to gains in the short run, it can ruin our reputation in the long run, which comes with a serious social cost.

people lied increased. At the end of the study we asked Leanora about her lying, and she said she was completely unaware that her lies were snowballing. She had habituated to her lies to such an extent that she did not even notice what had happened.

WHEN EMOTIONS FADE

Let's think back to the scenario we presented to you in the introduction. You are walking home one day and a large brown dog with sharp teeth barks at you, apparently in rage. Most likely you will feel a good amount of fear. The next day you pass by the same dog, and again it snarls at you. Only this time you don't feel as afraid as you did the day before. Fast-forward to a week later, and you hardly experience any emotional reaction to that dog's barks.

As you may remember, studies have shown that when people are initially presented with scary images, such as those of people shooting guns or of scary dogs, they exhibit a strong emotional response. Their heart rate increases, their pupils expand, and neurons in their amygdala fire. Yet, with each additional presentation of the same picture, their response decreases further and further, until it subsides altogether.[5]

Generally speaking, this form of habituation (which is sometimes referred to as emotional adaptation or emotional habituation) is a clever feature of the brain. Emotion is a signal that broadcasts, "This is important, take notice, you may need to react." But if something appears again and again without severely affecting us, it's probably not that important after all, which means that emotion can subside. Emotional habituation is not just about fear; you can adapt to any emotion, good or bad, such as love, excitement, and shame.

Leanora experienced such emotional habituation; it is why her emotional reaction decreased further and further every time she lied. Repeated dishonesty is like a Chanel perfume you apply over and over. At first you easily detect its distinctive scent every time you spritz. But over time and with repeated applications, you can hardly sense its presence, so you apply it more liberally, oblivious to why no one will sit by you on your morning commute. This happens because neurons in your olfactory bulb desensitize to the smell of the perfume.[6] Similarly, your emotional response to your own dishonesty is initially strong but decreases over time. Without a negative emotional reaction to your lies, you are more likely to lie.

If we gave you a pill that would magically extinguish your ability to feel emotion, you would likely lie more. This is not a hypothetical example. In an experiment a group of students about to take an exam were given pills called beta-blockers, which reduce emotional arousal; they were twice as likely to cheat compared to students who received a placebo![7] The medication artificially reduced that negative feeling that curbed cheating (a bit like the way habituation due to repeated lying does). Our moral nature, which most of us consider to be a deep reflection of who we are, seems to be modulated by biological functions that can be altered with a tiny pill.

THE POLITICS OF LIES

Jonah's repeated lying so as to conceal his missing toe triggered an effect similar to that of a beta-blocker. He no longer felt bad when fibbing and as a result did it more and more. Perhaps you can think of friends or family members who are in similar situations? Individuals in an extramarital affair who at first agonize over their actions, but after years of the cheating feel no remorse about it? Or others who lie repeatedly for social gain on social media or dating sites? Or those who tell frequent falsehoods to advance their careers? All these individuals likely habituate to their lying.

When Tali's study came out, just weeks before the 2016 presidential election in the United States, it hit a nerve. Many saw a connection between the findings and the behavior of the presidential candidate (and later president) Donald Trump, who was accused of repeated lying. Interestingly, fact-checking of his statements showed that in the first hundred days of his presidency he averaged almost five false public claims a day. That number nearly doubled months later, rising to nine a day, and reached over nineteen public false statements a day by the end of his term.[8]

Many factors may lie behind this continuous rise. Perhaps the increase is due to a reporting bias—that is, more of Trump's falsehoods may have been reported over time rather than more being actually uttered by him. Another possibility is that past lies needed to be covered up by more lies, causing a falsehood escalation. Or maybe lies led to personally beneficial consequences, leading to more and more lies. One study found that dishonesty pays off in politics: politicians who were not averse to lying were more likely to get reelected.[9] All these could cause lying to increase, but alongside all this, we suspect that in politics, as elsewhere, repeated lying triggers emotional habituation that enables more and more lies.

The picture becomes even more alarming when you consider that individuals may habituate not only to their own dishonesty but also to that of others. Politically speaking, this suggests that both voters and political advisers may become desensitized to a politician's falsehoods in the same way that they do to the overused Chanel perfume of their spouse, making them less likely to act to punish, and perhaps to stop, dishonest behavior. A politician may in turn interpret the absence of sanctions as a "green light." And so, as the number of falsehoods increases, less and less outrage may be observed from the public.

This is exactly what happened in the United States. After living through what has become known as the "post-truth era," the number of Americans who said it was fine to exaggerate facts to make a story more interesting grew from 44 percent in 2004 to a staggering 66 percent in 2018.[10]

Habituation to the lies of others is a problem you can find all around you, not just in politics. It happens in business, science, personal relationships, and social media. Imagine, for example, that you take a job as a content editor for a "wellness guru" named Belle. Your job is to copyedit content she writes and post it on her popular website and social media accounts. These accounts have millions of followers, so you are excited about your new job.

The first piece you receive from Belle is about the incred-ible healing properties of eggplants. Who knew the purple vegetable was especially therapeutic! Out of curiosity, you conduct a Google search, which reveals no evidence in sup-port of the claim. When you ask Belle about it, she explains that, yes, there is no evidence at present, but there may be evidence in the future. You do enjoy a good baba ghanoush, so you cross every *t* and dot every *i* and publish the piece.

The next day you receive a piece claiming that ostrich eggs, which are offered for sale on Belle's website, boost reproduc-tion (of humans, that is, not birds). While this sounds a bit off, you copyedit and publish the piece. Who knows? Maybe there is something to it. This kind of thing repeats each day.

A couple of months into the job, you get assigned a piece suggesting that "clean eating" is a more effective treatment for cancer than chemotherapy. Belle urges cancer patients to opt out of chemotherapy. This article, unlike those about eggplants or bird eggs, may have serious consequences for patients. Now imagine that you receive the same story, not two months into your job, but on your very first day. Under which scenario will you be more likely to edit and publish the article?

Because people are much more likely to engage in unethi-cal acts when such behavior gradually increases over time than when it emerges abruptly,[11] under the latter scenario you will be less likely to publish the piece. When ethical erosion is gradual, people are less likely to take notice and more likely to engage in wrongdoing. But when it comes out of nowhere, it is clear that a line is crossed, and people react accordingly. In other words, stories about therapeutic eggplants and reproduction-boosting bird eggs blur the line between what is true and what is false, what is acceptable and what is intolerable. It creates a new norm. When a much more troublesome situation arises, which under normal circumstances would be obviously objectionable, it appears far closer to the acceptance line than it would otherwise.

The foregoing example is not purely a product of our imagination. It is based on former Australian wellness guru Belle Gibson.[12] Gibson was a star "influencer." She had a popular healthy-eating app that was backed by Apple, a cookbook published by Penguin, and a large online following on Instagram, Facebook, and other social media platforms.

In her book and on her media accounts, Gibson informed her followers that she had cancer, which she was fighting with a healthy diet, physical exercise, meditation, and other alternative treatments. Her posts and blogs detailed her cancer journey, which she claimed was triggered by a cervical cancer vaccine. In her account, it had spread to her brain, spleen, uterus, liver, and kidneys.

She was managing it well, she said, by using natural remedies rather than chemotherapy. Gibson posted pictures of herself looking fit and healthy, so many were moved to adopt her routines. Some cancer patients were even persuaded to forgo conventional medicine.

Gibson's success grew exponentially for years, until one day an investigative journalist revealed it was all a big scam. Gibson never had brain cancer, nor did she have liver or kidney cancer. There were no records of her being diagnosed with any cancer whatsoever. She lied about her health, her age, and her finances. Money she claimed to have donated to charities from her company's profits was never received.

Unsurprisingly, Gibson had a track record of falsehoods going back to childhood. As a teenager she falsely claimed to have died momentarily on the operating table while undergoing heart surgery. She never had heart surgery. Her friends remember Gibson lying constantly. Those seemingly harmless childhood fibs grew over the years into lies that made her millions, while risking the health of her followers.[13]

A blueprint like Gibson's is detectable in many otherwise diverse stories of grand deceit that have become front-page news over the years. All of them—from Rachel Dolezal, who falsely claimed to be Black, and Elizabeth Holmes, who used fraudulent claims to build a biotechnology empire, to George Santos, the member of Congress who lied about his education and his employment, to behavioral scientist Diederik Alexander Stapel, who fabricated scientific data[14]—had one thing in common. Their dishonest acts could be traced back to a sequence of smaller transgressions that gradually escalated.

None of this is to say that people who find themselves in a position like Jonah's, in which they feel a need to lie repeatedly, will all end up committing serious crimes. Jonah himself grew up to be a good father and a respected member of society (although he never got rid of his lying habit). Nor are we saying that pretending to go to bed every night for the sake of domestic bliss will eventually lead to grand deceit. Numerous complex factors lead certain individuals to orchestrate the world's largest Ponzi scheme or to fake cancer, and many of them have nothing to do with habituation.

What we are saying is that small lies can and do lead to more frequent and larger lies. In the words of Bernard Madoff, "It starts out with you taking a little bit, maybe a few hundred, a few thousand. You get comfortable with that, and before you know it, it snowballs into something big."[15] This is true for the Holmeses and the Gibsons of this world, and it could be true for you too.

THE SELFLESS LIE

You might wonder whether dishonesty always escalates, or whether it matters if lies are told "for good reason." Consider the selfless lie, one that is told purely for the benefit of another person. Covering up for a colleague at work and taking the blame for a mistake a sibling committed are examples of selfless lying. People often don't feel too bad about such lies. They may feel virtuous and so have nothing to which to habituate.

In our coins-in-the-jar experiment, we created a situation in which advisers (such as Leanora) could lie to help the advisee (such as Rina) without any benefit to themselves. We found that people did lie for the benefit of others, even for complete strangers, but those lies did *not* escalate.

We also created another situation where lies would benefit both the liar *and* the other person. Here we found that lies did escalate, although not as dramatically as when people lied only for selfish reasons. We speculate that our volunteers felt a bit bad for lying, as they were doing it for their own benefit too, but the fact that it also benefited the other person softened those feelings.

Some of the most famous liars in recent times—including Gibson and Holmes—did benefit others. Their lies benefited their families and their employees. Gibson had a young son; Holmes provided jobs for company employees. Their lies gave hope to their followers and clients, though that hope turned out to be based on a scam.

Believing that your dishonesty aids others may make it seem justifiable. Yet it does not completely clear you of guilt, shame, and fear—at least not at the beginning of the journey. Think back to Madoff's words—"You get comfortable with that," he says, referring to lying.[16] Those words suggest that at some point he was *not* comfortable with it. Rather, he became comfortable with his scam over time.

This last point may distinguish psychopaths from the Madoffs of the world. Perhaps the Madoffs were uncomfortable with their act at first, while the psychopaths never were. They felt nothing from the very beginning.

NIP IT IN THE BUD?

Knowing that dishonesty escalates due to habituation has clear implications for how to decrease it at home and at work: nip it in the bud.

If you ignore small transgressions, they may slowly snowball to acts with serious consequences. People might get used to dishonesty and no longer consider it wrong. At home, calling out kids when they lie, so they feel remorse, may make them less likely to habituate to their own dishonesty. Such interventions will generate clear norms about what is tolerable and what isn't, before things get ugly.

In the workplace, you might well be better off and avoid much bigger problems by creating an atmosphere where minuscule lies (such as cheating by a few dollars on expenses) are not acceptable. This is how we run our own teams. Small transgressions are immediately addressed in order to deliver a clear message. We do this to avoid the possibility of larger transgressions (for example, scientific misconduct) in the future, which may lead to serious negative consequences, not just to the dishonest person, but to other people within and outside our team.

Norms are often rigid: do not lie (ever), do not steal (ever), do not be disrespectful toward your parents (ever), do not reveal confidential information (ever), do not break your promises (ever). The rigidity of the norms may seem a bit extreme, but that is the point. They ensure an intense emotional reaction that makes it more difficult for people to get comfortable with their moral transgressions.

Ordinary life offers many examples of things we consider egregious moral wrongs, and we will not do those things, even if there would be benefits from doing so. We will not take the first step. As possible examples, consider the following:[17]

- How much would you have to be paid to burn your nation's flag?
- How much would you have to be paid to kick a dog in the head, hard?
- How much would you have to be paid to slap your mother in the face?

· How much would you have to be paid to make cruel re-
marks to an overweight person about his or her appearance?

Many people say that no amount of money would be
enough. In a way, that seems absurd. If someone would pay
you a fortune to burn your nation's flag, you could use the
money to help people in need; you could even use the money
to promote patriotism (and to make a lot more flags). We are
aghast at the thought of kicking a dog in the head, hard, and
we are not sure whether we could do it (even if no one would
ever see or know we did), but what if the monetary reward
would save the lives of one hundred dogs, or ten thousand
dogs? You get the idea.

People think that some trade-offs are taboo and that some
values are "protected" or "sacred," which means that people
would be reluctant to violate them even if the rewards for
doing so are high and punishments nil.[18] Indeed, people report
intense negative emotions when they are asked to trade off certain values—as, for instance, when they are asked whether to
increase risks of death to some (as in the case of experimental
medical treatments) in the interest of decreasing risks to many.

Amid the COVID-19 pandemic, for example, a well-known
behavioral economist was hired to advise his government on
how to combat the spread of the disease. The economist sub-
mitted a report with an unusual recommendation: he advised
the government to infect an army base with the virus to closely
study the spread of the disease, examine symptoms, and quantify the effectiveness of different interventions. The economist

also shared his recommendation with the press.[19] His rationale was that while a few lives might be lost, many more were likely to be saved from the knowledge gained. Neither the government nor the citizens were impressed; the majority were outraged.

Economists tend to think that the whole idea of taboo trade-offs is a mystery, or a violation of basic rationality. But if we focus on habituation, the mystery might start to dissolve. A social norm against *ever* doing X or Y or Z, ensuring that people feel ashamed or terrible when they contemplate X or Y or Z, can stop people from starting on a path that could produce harm and horror. If a culture has a strong norm against lying or cheating, such that the very thought triggers intense negative emotions, it might protect itself against terrible things.

The philosopher Bernard Williams suggested that if people think about how to maximize utility in some moral dilemmas (such as whether to leap into the street to save a loved one), they are having "one thought too many." In his view, they should just do the right thing, without thinking much about it.[20] Williams meant to make a philosophical point about the foundations of morality. We do not know if he was right, but his claim makes a certain psychological sense. It might well be good if people just think "I will not lie" rather than "Lying isn't worth it in the particular circumstances, given all relevant costs and benefits."

THE INVENTION OF LYING

Where does all this leave a parent at 8:00 p.m. whose son becomes sleepy but resists turning in until his sister does too? A parent can't treat small lies as purely harmless. If we let small lies slide, people can get comfortable lying and will do so more often. That is doubly true for children, who are developing life-long habits. Nipping dishonesty in the bud can prevent it from escalating, so parents should resist encouraging minor acts of dishonesty. But truth be told, it's not always easy.

Imagine living in a world where people are unable to produce falsehoods. If your date is wearing an unflattering outfit, you tell him so. At a job interview, you candidly list your virtues and flaws. When selling a used car, you quote its exact worth. On Instagram you post only unfiltered photos. On the positive side, there are no "fakes," deep or shallow. But there is also no fiction, no storytelling, no Santa Claus or tooth fairies. What would such a world look like?[21]

The Invention of Lying, a film written by and starring Ricky Gervais, explores a world in which lying does not exist. When Gervais's character utters the first ever lie told by a human being, he is unsure how to describe what he has just done. The word *lie* does not exist, so the word *truth* has not been invented either. "I said something that . . . wasn't," he tries to explain. The film is not a cinematic triumph. But it's ingenious. It demonstrates the delicate balance between the necessity of little lies for maintaining a stable social milieu (e.g., telling your friend you are canceling at the last minute because of a cold rather than admitting you found something better to do), and the hazard of big lies that cause devastation (e.g., intentional falsehoods that lead to a war).

Nowadays the distinction between truths and lies seems to be fading. In some respects, lying has become an acceptable part of modern life, where with the click of a mouse you can build an alternate persona only loosely resembling yourself. As a result, you will often encounter falsehoods online, which contribute to a significant problem in the modern world—misinformation.

7

(MIS)INFORMATION:
HOW TO MAKE PEOPLE BELIEVE
(ALMOST) ANYTHING

*Slogans should be persistently repeated until the
very last individual has come to grasp the idea.*

—ADOLF HITLER[*][1]

I F YOU MEASURE SIZE by population, New York is the largest
state in the United States. Led by New York City—the most
populous city in the world—New York has a host of highly pop-
ulated cities, including Buffalo, Rochester, Yonkers, Syracuse,
Albany, Mount Vernon, Utica, and White Plains. Though New
York is the nation's largest state by population, it is not the

---

[*] Some may think Hitler should not be quoted. We completely understand this
view. It is also instructive, however, to be aware of, and highlight, his thinking,
and the psychological principles on which he relied to sway his followers. Remembering what he did, and making the dangers of his tactics salient, may help
to keep history from being repeated. We recommend here Géraldine Schwarz,
Those Who Forget (2020).

largest by total area. That honor goes to California. Remarkably, the state with the largest population is only the eighth largest by area, behind California, Alaska, Texas, Montana, New Mexico, Oregon, and New Hampshire.

The paragraph you just read is full of falsehoods. New York is not the most populous state in the United States. California wins that prize, followed by Texas and then Florida; New York is fourth. Yet because we told you (three times, no less) that New York is the most populous state in the United States, you might well be inclined to believe it. Whenever a falsehood is repeated, people tend to think that it is true. As we will soon explain, this is partly because when a statement is repeated again and again, your brain processes it less and less as it is no longer surprising or new. The result is that you are more likely to accept it as a given.

At this point you might be thinking, "Wait, you just told me that New York is *not* the most populous state in the United States. So going forward I'm never going to think it is!" Don't be so sure. We'll get to that later.

Psychologists have a name for the tendency to believe repeated statements: the *illusory truth effect*.[2] It is why many people believe that humans use only 10 percent of their brain and that vitamin C can prevent the common cold (Tali is unable to shake off this latter belief). The phenomenon was discovered back in 1977 when a group of psychologists asked volunteers in a study how confident they were about the truth of sixty plausible (but not necessarily true) statements.[3]

Try it yourself—do you think the statements below are true or false?

- The People's Republic of China was founded in 1947.
- The Louvre in Paris is the largest museum in the world.
- Cairo, Egypt, has a larger population than Chicago, Illinois.
- The thigh bone is the longest bone in the human body.
- In the United States, divorced people outnumber those who are widowed.
- Lithium is the lightest of all metals.

The volunteers rated the statements on three different occasions at two-week intervals. Twenty of the statements (including both false and true ones) were repeated across the sessions. The other forty were not. Sure enough, people were much more likely to believe that statements were correct if they were repeated! It seems that if you repeat a statement enough times (for example, "Going out in the cold with wet hair will make you sick," or "Space aliens landed in Roswell, New Mexico, in the 1940s"), people might start believing it.

Scientists have repeated this particular statement on countless occasions, so we might be especially inclined to think that it is real. But it is, in fact, real. Since 1977, the illusory truth effect has been found in numerous independent studies. It has been found outside the laboratory with members of the general public.[4] It has been found with short rather than long intervals between repetitions.[5] It has been found with factual statements of very different kinds—historical events, geography, science, politics, art, literature.[6]

You might be wondering if everyone is vulnerable to the illusory truth effect. Surely some of us aren't, you might think. Do professors, scientists, engineers, teachers, journalists, acrobats, and astronauts all fall for it? The answer is yes.[7] You might expect that the effect would be reduced among people who rely on analytical rather than intuitive thinking—and who like to think in terms of numbers and data. But you would be wrong: analytical thinkers are not less subject to the effect. Or you might think that young people would be especially prone to the illusory truth effect—or perhaps old people would be especially prone to it. Wrong again. Young people and old people are equally prone to it.

Or you might predict that people with a lot of cognitive ability (e.g., people who score well on general intelligence tests, and who can process information easily and well) would be less likely to fall prey to it. That prediction would also be wrong. Or you might predict that people with a high need for "cognitive closure," who want firm, clear answers to questions, would be especially likely to show the effect. But that too would be wrong.

The illusory truth effect appears to be a feature of all minds—bright or dull, fresh or wrinkled.[8] There is one exception, though—people with Alzheimer's disease seem not to be affected as much by repetition.[9] This is probably because they have no memory of what they previously heard.

FAMILIAR, TRUTHIER

Let's not overstate these findings. You are unlikely to believe false statements if you are confident that they are false. If you are repeatedly told that the earth is flat or that the Holocaust never happened, you are not necessarily going to believe either of those statements even if you hear them repeatedly (although some people do). The point is simply that repetition can make people think that a proposition is more likely to be true, whether or not it is—so if someone wants to convince you of a falsehood, stating it over and over, and then once more, might actually do the trick. (Hitler knew that, and so do some commentators on television, and so do some "influencers" on social media.) The interesting question is: Why?

The answer is that repetition creates a feeling of familiarity. And when something sounds familiar, you assume it is true. This is because in life a feeling of familiarity is often (rightly) associated with truth, and a feeling of surprise is often (rightly) associated with implausibility. Imagine, for example, that we told you that we own a rainbow-colored cat that speaks Swedish. To put it mildly, you would feel *surprised*. That feeling is a good indicator that something is not right, and that you should slow down and carefully consider the statement.[10]

You would then likely compare the statement to your existing knowledge—cats are rarely colorful and communicate only with meows—which would lead to the conclusion that our statement is likely false! All this happens in a split second. You are not even aware of it. Now, if we told you we owned a brown cat that meows when he wants to eat, we would produce a comfortable feeling of familiarity. That feeling will translate to "Yeah, sounds about right."

When you have heard a statement many times before, you take it for granted and respond to it less—you are habituated to it. It does not produce surprise. But when you hear an unfamiliar statement, you feel jarred and so you question it.

It makes sense to be inclined to believe a statement that sounds familiar and to be skeptical when a statement sounds surprising. In general, familiar-sounding statements *are* more likely to be true. This is because you have heard familiar statements from different sources—maybe from your mom and your friend Ellen, and on the news. If all these people agree, then the statement is likely correct (you might reasonably think). So a "familiar, truthier" heuristic is not bad. The problem arises when untruths become familiar due to repetition, either because people have the wrong idea or because they are trying to spread false information.

The source of the problem is that your brain is pretty good at indicating "I heard this before" (i.e., this is "familiar"), but not as good at remembering where you heard this before, from whom, and in what context.[11] Storing all that extra information takes effort and requires valuable resources. When you hear, "Vitamin C can help treat the common cold," you know that you have heard the statement before, but you do not necessarily recall if you heard it from your superstitious uncle or a trusted scientist. Nevertheless, the familiar, truthier heuristic kicks in.

Just hearing part of a statement, such as "House mice can run," makes it more likely that you will believe the full statement: "House mice can run forty miles per hour." Being exposed to the first few words makes you feel as if you have been exposed to the whole statement, which in turn gives you a sense of familiarity, which in turn triggers the familiar, truthier heuristic.[12]

This is why repeating a statement to debunk it can backfire. Imagine that your Facebook friend Pinocchio posts, "Most inmates in the U.S. are immigrants." You look this up and find it is untrue, so you post, "It is untrue that most inmates in the U.S. are immigrants." Now your other friend Geppetto scrolls through his feed and encounters both posts. The phrase "most inmates in the U.S. are immigrants" becomes familiar to him because of repetition and therefore *feels* true. Geppetto does not remember your negation, only the basic claim.

Geppetto, like most of us, is highly attuned to primary information: whether the weather report says that it is going to be cold today, whether a candidate for public office claims that he was a war hero, whether the local newspaper reports that a famous television star committed a drug offense. By contrast, Geppetto is less attuned to "meta-information," meaning information about whether primary information is accurate. If you are clearly told that the supposed weather report was a joke, or that a public official is distorting his record to attract votes, you won't exactly ignore that. But if you're like Geppetto (and most people), you will give it less weight than you should. If you like psychological terms, this one is known as *metacognitive myopia*.[13]

What all this means is that you need to be careful not to repeat falsehoods even if it is to debunk them. Sometimes it is best to ignore a falsehood altogether to avoid giving it traction. To be sure, sometimes falsehoods need to be addressed head-on. But even in those situations, you should avoid repeating the misinformation and instead lay out the facts.

For example, which do you think would be a better statement to post if you are trying to refute Pinocchio's post that "most inmates in the U.S. are immigrants"?

A. "Fewer than 10 percent of inmates in the U.S. are immigrants."

B. "91 percent of inmates in the U.S. were born in the U.S."

At their core, both statements convey the same idea. However, statement A ties together the word *immigrants* with *inmates* in people's minds. Associating these two concepts may unintentionally trigger a familiarity signal when people hear "most inmates in the U.S. are immigrants" a few weeks later, which may cause the statement to seem valid. Statement B avoids that pitfall.

EASIER, TRUTHIER

When you have heard something over and over, it feels familiar, and you might well believe that it must be true. But that is not the only reason repetition leads you to accept claims. There is more to it.

Let's say you are exposed to a piece of information for the first time—for example, "a shrimp's heart is in its head." If so, your brain will spend a good amount of energy processing this nugget. You may try to imagine the heart in the head, or you may try to recall the last time you ate shrimp. The next time you are exposed to the same piece of information ("a shrimp's heart is in its head"), your brain does not need to do much work, so it responds less. The third time ("a shrimp's heart is in its head"), even less and even faster.[14] This is a form of habituation. Just as your brain stops responding to the smell of your aftershave after repeated use, so it stops responding to the claim "a shrimp's heart is in its head."

To be clear, we are not saying that the same neural mechanism that desensitizes you to your own aftershave also causes you to believe repeated information. What we are saying is that the basic principle—namely, that *neural processing is reduced in response to repeated stimuli*—is at work in both cases. When it is effortless for you to process information because of repetition (i.e., less neural response), you are more likely to accept it as true. Effortless means there is no "surprise signal." You don't stop to ponder; you just accept.

We don't even need to repeat the exact same statement for this energy-saving to happen. For example, because we have told you many times now that "a shrimp's heart is in its head," you will be more likely to accept that "a shrimp's heart is in its head and its brain is in its rectum." As you heard the first half of the sentence before ("a shrimp's heart is in its head"), fewer resources are needed to process the whole sentence ("a shrimp's heart is in its head and its brain is in its rectum"). The information as a whole becomes easier to process, which triggers a sense of familiarity, which translates to belief.

(To set the record straight: Shrimp *do* have their heart and other critical organs, such as their stomach, in their head. This is because their head has a protective shell that is stronger than the rest of their body. Their brain, however, is not in their rectum; it too is in their head.)

Repeating statements again and again is one way to make information easier to process (which corresponds to less in the way of neural response to the information), but it's not the only way. For example, which of the following two statements do you think is true?

(i) **Playing classical music to unborn babies increases their IQ.**

(ii) Eating peanuts when pregnant increases the chances the baby will be allergic to them.

If you are like most people, you will be more likely to believe that the first statement is true. (In fact, neither is true.) Because the first statement is printed in a slightly larger font than the second, it is easier to process. Information that is easier to process—perhaps because it is printed in salient colors such as red or in easy-to-read fonts—is more likely to be believed.[15] You associate the ease with which information is processed with its truthfulness. (Easier, truthier!) We use the word *associate* for a reason: you don't really *think* that information is more likely to be true if it is easier to process. It's a matter of association. We tend automatically to believe information more if it can be easily processed.

It follows that if you are presenting information at work or on social media, and it is in a small font or a poorly contrasting color, people are less likely to believe it. And if the statement sounds completely new, people are going to be even more skeptical. To help people trust your recommendations, make content easy to process. Make it visually easier (add pictures, use big fonts, high contrast) and conceptually easier (tie the idea to concepts that are familiar, prime people for what you are about to say, repeat!). Avoid making people skeptical of your work simply because they find it hard to process.

REPEAT, BELIEVE, SPREAD

Knowledge of the illusory truth effect can help you communicate and share critical information with others. This is all well and good if you are sharing accurate information. But many people, including politicians and marketers, make a point of repeating false or unsubstantiated claims. For example, many ads repeat shaky claims about a product ("wearable stickers made from space-suit material promote healing"), as this can cause potential buyers to believe it merely by virtue of repetition, or perhaps to think they heard the claim from a reliable source before, thus increasing sales. Or politicians may repeat a baseless claim with an understanding that if they say it often enough, people will start to think that it is true. Even Adolf Hitler grasped this concept. In *Mein Kampf* he wrote, "Slogans should be persistently repeated until the very last individual has come to grasp the idea."[16]

To protect the marketplace, regulators enforce bans on deceptive advertising, but they have yet to catch up with the impact of repetition. A false statement should be punished more severely if it is frequently repeated. Or consider social media. Those who run Meta, X, YouTube, and the like have yet to come to terms with the potentially destructive power of repetition. Might the problem be not only that encountering a post repeatedly increases the belief in its accuracy via habituation, but also that it increases the likelihood that it will be further shared? To study this question Tali conducted an experiment.[17]

Tali's collaborator on this experiment—Valentina Vellani—showed a few hundred participants a list of sixty statements about geography, science, history, health (such as "Caffeine consumption reduces bone growth in kids"), and more. Half the statements were shown twice and half only once. As you would by now expect, the volunteers were more likely to believe the statements that were shown twice than those shown only once (the illusory truth effect at work). Then Valentina asked the volunteers which statements they would like to share on a Twitter account.

Lo and behold, the participants were more likely to want to share those statements they observed twice than those they observed only once. Valentina wondered whether repeated statements were more often shared because her participants believed them to be true. To answer this question, she conducted a statistical analysis (known as *mediation modeling*). The analysis was consistent with her hunch that repeated headlines will indeed be shared more often because people believe them to be true.

This suggests that most people are not trying to mislead anyone. To the contrary, most prefer to share information they *believe* is accurate. The problem is simply that repetition leads people to be mistaken about what is true. This problem is not at all new. It is a modern manifestation of an old predicament.

A TRUTH BIAS

In the fall of 1934, sales of Chesterfield cigarettes declined sharply due to growing health concerns. It was not the fear of lung cancer that drove people away from the brand. The relationship between smoking and cancer was not even suspected until the 1940s. People stopped buying Chesterfields because they were scared of . . . leprosy.[18] Leprosy is an infectious disease that causes large disfiguring skin sores and extensive nerve damage to the limbs. It is both rare and treatable today, but it was a grave concern in the 1930s.

Why would people think that smoking Chesterfield cigarettes causes leprosy? Well, a rumor circulated that a leper was working in the Chesterfield factory in Richmond, Virginia. According to the story, anyone who smoked Chesterfields was at risk of catching the terrible disease. Despite the lack of cell phones, emails, and social media, the tale spread across the country like wildfire. The result? People turned to other brands.

The makers of Chesterfield tried to fight the rumor with all their might. They ran ads showing their sparkling-clean machines at work. They convinced the trusted mayor of Richmond to issue an official statement: "The Chesterfield factory had been examined and no leper was found." Alas, the attempts were fruitless. Sales continued to plummet and did not bounce back for a whole decade. No one knows exactly how the rumor started, but the makers of Chesterfield suspected their competitors made it up to gain a share of Chesterfield's market.

In many ways the Chesterfield story is a classic case of misinformation escalation. The rumor evoked both curiosity and fear, which caused people to pay attention and share the information with others. Repetition then increased people's belief in the rumor (partially because ease of processing increased), which increased the likelihood that it would be shared further.

People believed the leper story for another reason, on which we have yet to touch: "the truth bias."[19] The truth bias is the basic human tendency to believe what we are told. We tend to assume that others are telling the truth because they usually are. Suppose, for example, that you are in a new town and you ask strangers for directions. It will probably not cross your mind that they are trying to get you lost. In general, trusting others is necessary for a functioning society. It would be impossible to live in a world in which everyone assumes everyone else is lying.

But the truth bias can get us in real trouble, as evidenced by the billions of dollars lost every year to phishing scams and other incidents of fraud. Again, it's not only the tech illiterate, the elderly, or teenagers who fall for the truth bias and therefore for scams. Many savvy businesspeople, and sophisticated people of all other kinds, have been victims.

Consider the well-publicized case of Anna Sorokin, who pretended to be a wealthy German heiress and who defrauded major New York investors, banks, and hotels for large sums of money. Or consider a case in which *New York Times* bestselling authors were scammed into emailing their soon-to-be-published manuscripts to a man pretending to be their editor's assistant.

———

Many years ago Tali found herself a victim of the truth bias. Tali was a student living in central London. She would often sublet her apartment while traveling abroad to conferences and workshops. One evening she returned from a weeklong trip to DC, where she'd attended a conference. Exhausted from the long flight, she was eager to take a shower and get straight to bed. Alas, when she tried to unlock the door, her keys would not fit. "That's strange," she thought, and tried again, but to no avail. Her surprise turned to alarm when she heard voices from inside her apartment: *"Chi è la? Chi è la?"* A woman in her thirties opened the door, a cigarette in one hand and a glass of white wine in the other: *"Sì?"*

The next moments are now a bit of a blur, but Tali explained, perhaps not calmly, that this was her apartment and who the hell were they? "Aha! We were waiting for you," said the woman, in a thick Italian accent. The Italian couple had rented the apartment from Tali's subletter, who told them the place was his and they could have it for six months—first and last month's rent up front, please. A day after they moved in, a Spanish man in his fifties showed up with suitcases and keys. He too had rented the apartment from the subletter and paid the first and last month's rent up front. The "owner" was no longer answering emails or phone calls, so the three went to the police. They realized the "owner" was a fraudster and they had, unfortunately, been scammed. They were not quite sure when or if the rightful owner would return, so they had decided to stay in the flat for the time being, changing the locks in case others attempted to move in.

That same night, the Italians moved out and Tali slept with a sofa shoved up against the door. The next morning, she discovered many of her belongings had vanished. The scammer took valuables such as a laptop and a camera and, even more devastatingly, personal items such as clothes, DVDs (yes, this was a while ago), books, and canvas paintings.

As Tali looked back, the clues were not subtle. The scammer never came by to view the flat. "I only need it for a few hours here and there between meetings in the city," he said. When Tali warned him that the shower was not working well (British plumbing), he claimed he was not planning on washing. ("Men," thought Tali.) The guy paid in cash, which he insisted on handing to Tali at 9:30 p.m. in an alley that was (conveniently) unlit, so Tali could not make out his facial features.

The default assumption of truth is so robust that it can override strong clues of lying. Tali did have a bad gut feeling, especially while standing in the dark alley exchanging keys for cash, but those feelings were dismissed in favor of the default.

Studies show that even when information is discredited (as in the Chesterfield case) or explicitly said to be false, we may still rely on it to guide our choices.[20] Is this the case even when your profession is, by definition, to uncover the truth?

To find out, a group of researchers headed by a scholar by the name of Myrto Pantazi recruited experienced judges and gave them information on criminal defendants in two legal cases.[21] The judges were explicitly told that some of this information was false. They were then asked to assess how dangerous the defendants were and to come up with appropriate prison terms. Would the judges adequately discount information that they were told was false?

The answer is that they did not. When they received negative information about the defendant, they were influenced by it, even when they had been explicitly informed that it was not true. That's not all. They also tended to misremember false evidence as being true, and they did so more often than they remembered true evidence as being false. Amazingly, even if you are an experienced judge, false information about a criminal defendant might well affect your conclusions—even when you are explicitly told it is false.

INCENTIVIZE ACCURACY

The combination of the truth bias and the easier, truthier heuristic can make us vulnerable to misinformation, fake news, and scams. But knowledge of these biases and heuristics also gives us power. We cannot override them, as they are well ingrained in the architecture of our brains, but once we are aware of them, we can put policies in place to protect ourselves. Following the London incident, Tali did thorough background checks before committing to any sizable transaction. More aggressive falsehood-countering policies should be put in place not only by individuals, but also by companies, including social media platforms, to protect society. Technology and media platforms often amplify our basic human tendency to assume that people are telling the truth, and to believe and share repeated information even when it is false.

It does not need to be this way. Science has something to say about what we can do. A study published in the journal *Nature* showed that prompting users to consider the veracity of just a single statement shifted their mindset, such that they became more sensitive to accuracy.[22] As a consequence, the number of reliable news links people shared relative to fake news links tripled.

Another approach may be to reward users for reliability. Imagine if people were rewarded online when they posted accurate information on a social media platform and were punished when they posted falsehoods.[23] Would this carrot-and-stick system reduce the spread of misinformation?

Tali and her colleagues Laura Globig and Nora Holtz tested this idea.[24] As we see it, one problem with social media platforms is that rewards, in the form of likes, retweets, and such, are not contingent on accuracy. That means that you can post something completely false and receive thousands of likes. So you learn that posting false information is an easy way to get attention. But what if we made just a tiny change to the incentive structure of social media platforms to explicitly provide visible rewards to reliable users?

Tali and her team did just that. They created a social media platform that was in many ways similar to Twitter but added two new buttons to the traditional mix: *trust* and *distrust*. Three things happened. First, users clicked *trust* and *distrust* to separate true from false posts three times more than other buttons such as *like*. This was the case for Democrats and for Republicans and across many domains (science, politics, health). Second, users started posting more true than false posts. Why?

They wanted to receive as many trust "carrots" as possible and avoid those horrible distrust "sticks." As a result, the spread of misinformation was cut by half. But that's not all. Third, users ended up with more accurate beliefs. Why? Maybe because they spent more time and effort pondering what is true and what is false in an attempt to get positive feedback.

The study was not carried out on real social media platforms (for that we need the Musks and Zuckerbergs of the world to get involved), so we cannot guarantee it would work. But we think it is worth a try, especially if our goal is to create a society where the truth bias is no longer a bias at all.

PART III

HEALTH AND SAFETY

8

RISK:

WHAT THE SWEDES TAUGHT US ON HÖGERTRAFIKOMLÄGGNINGEN

*My comfort zone is like a little bubble around me, and
I've pushed it in different directions and made it bigger
and bigger until these objectives that seemed totally
crazy eventually fall within the realm of the possible.*

—ALEX HONNOLD, ROCK CLIMBER[1]

JOE BURRUS WAS LYING in a wooden coffin a few feet underground. This is not unusual; most of us will end up in a casket. Except that Joe could hear his family and friends aboveground. He was alive.

It was Oregon, 1989, and Joe, also known as Amazing Joe, was attempting a stunt made famous by the great Harry Houdini. In 1915 Houdini was buried alive six feet under. Houdini's mission was to dig himself out. But the task turned out to be much harder than he ever imagined. With every inch of dirt, he had to fight for his life. When at last the tip of his hand emerged above the surface, he lost consciousness. Luckily his assistants were able to drag him out just in time, saving his life.[2]

Joe believed he could do better. "I consider myself a master of illusion and an escape artist," he said. "I believe I'm the next Houdini and greater."[3] On that day in Oregon, Joe did manage to undo the handcuffs that tied his wrists, get out of the coffin, and dig through the dirt to the surface, where he met his adoring fans. The stunt was a huge success. So Joe decided to do it again a year later.

On Halloween Eve 1990, Joe was in Blackbeard's Family Entertainment Center in Fresno, California. Once again, he was lying inside a coffin. Except this time, he selected a clear plastic-and-glass box. The plastic was not as strong as the wood, but the see-through coffin would allow the audience to observe Joe as he descended into his grave. The grave was seven feet deep—deeper than the one he had emerged from the year prior, and deeper than the hole that almost took Houdini's life. In 1989 Joe's coffin was covered with dirt. This time, Joe added cement to the mix. This meant he would have to free himself from handcuffs, escape a plastic coffin, and dig through seven feet of dirt and cement.[4]

The risk was inordinate. Yet Joe believed he could escape. He was not deterred by the warnings of family, friends, journalists, and colleagues. He was so confident that even a fracture discovered at the corner of the box did not stop him. He taped it with duct tape.

This story does not end well. Shortly after nine tons of dirt and cement were poured on top of Joe, a crack was heard as the plastic coffin gave way to the massive weight of the cement. It buried him alive.

Many factors led Joe to the decision that would eventually take his life. But one factor that likely played a role affects us all: *risk habituation*, which is the tendency to perceive a behavior as less and less risky the more you engage in it, even though the actual threat remains the same. You find yourself taking greater and greater risks[5] while feeling less and less scared.

As we will soon see, risk habituation can cause politicians to make decisions that will destroy their careers and harm their country, can trigger reckless driving, and can lead workers to take unnecessary risks on the job. Risk habituation affects decisions related to your safety, your health, and your finances.

For a glimpse, consider a study that Tali conducted with Hadeel Haj Ali.[6] In that study, volunteers played twenty games of roulette over and over. Not until the very end would the volunteers learn if they had won or lost. Tali and Hadeel found that at the beginning volunteers gambled just a little bit, but over time they seemed to become more comfortable and gambled larger and larger amounts. The financial risk they took escalated. While in this study the maximum amount they were allowed to gamble was relatively modest, you can imagine how similar risk escalation can lead gamblers to lose a lot of money in the real world, including in the stock market (which is a gamble, after all). That is a problem.

Still, habituating to risk allows us to push boundaries, to live both richer and calmer lives, and to progress as individuals and as a species. To see how to balance the upside with the downside, let's get familiar with risk habituation.

RISK HABITUATION

Imagine that you are hiking in the woods when you reach a beautiful bridge over a serene blue pond. It is a hot day, and so, despite the risk, you decide to jump off the bridge to cool down in the pond. Your heart is thumping; the jump seems terrifying. But luckily you land safely in the fresh water and decide to go right back up and try again. This time your heart does not pound as fast, and you are not as cautious. It seems perfectly safe.

By the tenth jump you are attempting backflips. Unbeknownst to you, one in a hundred people who jump off this bridge ends up in the emergency room. Given those odds, it is not surprising that you landed safely in the water, but by jumping again and again, taking greater and greater risk, you are putting yourself in real danger.

To assess risk, people often rely on their feelings.[7] When you are about to do something risky—something that could result in a really good or a really bad outcome—you usually experience a surge of emotions, including fear, excitement, and arousal. Suppose that you are about to invest a large amount of money in Bitcoin, ask beautiful Catharine on a date, skydive, get on a roller coaster, or take cocaine. You will feel your heart race and your feet shake. Your brain interprets those signals to mean that the act is quite risky. Such feelings can serve as an internal brake, and perhaps you will refrain from jumping. If you feel nothing, there will be no brakes to stop you from going ahead. You might as well invest much more, ask Catharine to marry you, or jump off a cliff.

By now you are familiar with emotional habituation: if something triggers an emotional reaction within you, it will do so less and less every time you encounter it. So, the fear you feel before taking a risk—such as by jumping off the bridge—is reduced each time you do it. This is true as long as these past risky acts did not lead to disaster (that is, you landed safely in the blue water rather than breaking your skull). If you end up with cracked bones, you will dishabituate immediately.

So suppose that you take a risk: crossing a street on a snowy night, jumping off a bridge, texting and driving, having unprotected sex, exceeding the speed limit, investing in high-risk stocks, or burying yourself alive. If nothing bad happens, your brain will start to estimate the risk as lower than it did initially. After all, everything turned out fine. As a result, you are more likely to engage in the same behavior again and again and feel perfectly comfortable taking on larger and larger risks.

Now, this is not necessarily irrational. It is not crazy to estimate your risk by reference to your past experiences. You are updating your beliefs. But you don't have much data on which to rely. You are relying on a small number of personal experiences that happened to go well, often leading to overconfidence.

Let's think back to Joe Burrus. Joe did not wake up one morning and decide to bury himself alive in a plastic casket under tons of cement. On the contrary, he had several years of experience escaping a range of boxes in a range of situations. So he felt quite comfortable getting inside a casket. He felt so comfortable that the next logical step seemed to be doing so underground. Once he escaped from a few feet under, the idea of doing it again, this time with cement on top, appeared reasonable to him. Joe took more and more risk, and each time his perception of the risk was further divorced from the truth.

History is crowded with figures who took greater and greater risks, until the largest one exploded in their face. Take former British prime minister David Cameron. In the words of historian Anthony Seldon, "David Cameron will be remembered as a giant risk-taker, taking Britain to war in Libya in 2011, and failing to do so in Syria in 2013, calling the Scottish independence referendum in 2014 and the EU referendum in 2016.... It is still that decision to call the EU referendum that looms largest, as one of the greatest gambles in political history."[8]

Cameron believed that the referendum was a safe bet. Surely the British people would vote for Britain to remain in the European Union and thus weaken the power of his opponents. Well, that did not happen. Cameron's gamble ended his political career at the age of fifty and changed the course of British history.

People take larger and larger risks for many reasons beyond habituation. Escape artists might get larger and larger economic rewards for their feats. Politicians might need to take larger and larger risks to stay in office. It is likely, however, that habituation plays a major role.

OLD HAT, NEW HAT

For most of us, underestimating political risks or the danger of live burial is not an issue. Yet a bit of David Cameron and Joe Burrus is in all of us.

Consider COVID-19. When the lockdown was first initiated, Tali and her colleagues asked a large group of people whether they thought they would get infected and how dangerous they thought the virus was.[9] People thought that the risk was high; they were afraid and cautious. Tali then asked them again only a few weeks later (long before vaccines were introduced). People had become more and more relaxed, believing that the risk was not as great as they had previously thought. While the risk did not change much in the first few weeks, people gained experience in living with the threat and they got accustomed to hearing about cases. While the number of deaths mounted, people experienced the virus firsthand as mostly mild.

As a result, the majority were more likely to do things that put them in danger of infection. To be sure, some people exaggerated the risk to begin with, while others underestimated it. But the overall pattern was desensitization.

Being more alarmed by new and unfamiliar risks than by old and familiar ones is common,[10] and it need not be irrational. As we have said, people should learn from experience. Recall, however, that experience is limited and may not convey the whole story. We often get unduly scared by relatively new risks that are not such a big deal (think about genetically modified food) and are often not bothered by old risks that kill a lot of people (think about driving or unhealthy eating).

The general phenomenon—"scared by the new, bold with the old"—is an outgrowth of risk habituation. As the new and unfamiliar risk becomes old hat, people may treat it as smaller than it actually is. Habituation is one of many reasons why experienced investors carry more risky investment portfolios than do less experienced investors.[11]

The same trend is observed on construction sites and other work settings. Most accidents happen late in a project rather than early on.[12] As the days pass, workers habituate. They feel less and less fear, so they take fewer precautions.

Journalist Neil Swidey tells the extraordinary story of the decade-long Boston Harbor cleanup.[13] If you visit Boston Harbor today, you will be met by stunning, clear-blue waters, peppered with white sailing boats. But only a few decades ago, the harbor was the dirtiest in the United States. The polluted waters were peppered with debris. The harbor's makeover was a complex engineering feat employing hundreds of workers and costing $4 billion. It also took the lives of several men, all killed during the late stages of the project.

A high-risk mission at the completion of the ten-year project led to two of the deaths. Five divers were sent into a tube hundreds of feet below the ocean floor to remove heavy safety plugs. The tunnel had no oxygen or light and at its narrowest was only five feet in diameter. The divers were to travel all the way to the far end of the ten-mile-long tunnel and then inside a series of pipes only thirty inches wide.

Despite the complexity of the project, the divers trained for it for only two weeks and relied on an experimental breathing apparatus. The breathing system failed and only three of the divers got to safety, and with only thirty seconds to spare.

The tragedy, according to Swidey, occurred because the project manager and team accepted low standards of safety.

They did so even though the same manager and team had demonstrated flawless judgment and caution for the previous ten years. Seeing the end in sight, and having experienced no bad outcomes, they had a distorted perception of risk.

"We all know examples of a sawyer in a sawmill who has lost some fingers. This usually happens to those who have many years of experience and in the meantime have lost their risk sensitivity," says safety expert Juni Daalmans.[14] As Daalmans explains, you do not need to be a sawyer, diver, or magician to experience the new-hat, old-hat transformation; you probably experience it at home. "Habituation is one of the main reasons why the risk sensitivity at home generally is so low. A lot of accidents happen in the domestic environment because we are too complacent." As he puts it, "The fact that 50 percent of serious accidents occur in the domestic environment is a direct result of habituation."[15]

Risk habituation affects us all—in the kitchen, on the playground, in the pool, and on the roads, where more than thirty-eight thousand Americans die every year. Many drivers are less careful than they should be because they have gone a long time without an accident.

What can we do to overcome the problem?

HÖGERTRAFIKOMLÄGGNINGEN, OR "SHAKE IT UP"

At exactly 4:50 a.m. on Sunday, September 3, 1967, traffic in Sweden stopped. Cars, trucks, buses, motorcycles, and bicycles all came to a complete halt—and then carefully moved to the opposite side of the road.

The day is known as Högertrafikomläggningen, which translates to "the right-hand traffic diversion," or H-day for short. It was the day Sweden changed from driving on the left side of the road to the right. The move was initiated to align Sweden with the other Scandinavian countries. The fear was that drivers would get confused, turning the wrong way or getting too close to other cars when attempting to overtake them. That would seem to be a perfectly reasonable fear. Surprisingly, however, the switch did not result in a rise in motor accidents. On the contrary, the number of accidents and fatalities plunged! The number of motor insurance claims went down by 40 percent.[16]

What caused this reduction? you might well wonder. Perhaps it's safer to drive on the right side of the road than the left? But that cannot be the answer, as the miraculous improvement lasted for only two years. It seems that the main cause was risk *dis*habituation.[17]

If you pluck people out of the environment to which they are accustomed, perceptions of risk will be reset. This is exactly what happened on H-day. After the sudden switch from the left side to the right side of the road, people perceived the risk of being in a motor accident as high. They therefore drove with extreme caution, and fewer people got into accidents. After a period, people habituated again, and the number of accidents returned to normal. But for twenty-four months, the reduction in accidents translated to many lives saved.

There is a general lesson here. If you want to dishabituate people to a certain risk—your teenage son, your employees, yourself—you need to "shake it up." Every so often change the environment, alter the context, so that people move out of their comfort zone. For example, change the position to which employees are assigned when working on a conveyer belt or alter the colors of the warning signs on a construction site. By moving things around ever so slightly, you increase attention and alter risk perception.

In its 2020 regulation, the U.S. Food and Drug Administration (FDA) required that its various graphic warnings about the risks of cigarette smoking (the increased likelihood of cancer, heart disease, and so forth) be rotated quarterly.[18] Suppose that you see a graphic warning depicting someone in a hospital with lung cancer. The warning might scare you that first time, or even the first five times. But after a while, you might habituate. The depiction might become like background noise. That was exactly the FDA's concern. It believed that rotation of the various warnings was likely to reduce habituation and capture attention. So the solution was to portray someone in a hospital with lung cancer for a certain period, but then someone with rotting yellow teeth next, and so on.

A similar approach had been tested with online security pop-up warnings.[19] You are probably familiar with these pop-ups; you are trying to get access to lookagainbook.com, and a message appears telling you of problems with encryption and authentication protocols. This means that by accessing the site you may be allowing others to steal your data, including emails, texts, bank account details, credit card numbers, photos, and so forth. Many people ignore these warnings and access the site regardless. IT security experts believe that one explanation for this behavior is that people have habituated to such security warnings. Because the warnings appear so often, users do not even register them anymore.

To look into this problem, researchers at Google, the University of Pittsburgh, and Brigham Young University recorded the brain activity of people who observed a series of pop-up warnings.[20] They found that the first time a pop-up warning appeared, activity in the visual cortex, which processes visual stimuli, was strong. The second time the same warning appeared, visual activity dropped significantly, the third time saw a further drop, and so on. Classic neural adaptation.

So, the research team decided to, literally, shake it up.[21] They took the warnings and twirled them, jiggled them, zoomed in and out. This reduced neural adaptation. Not only was there less of a drop in visual activity, but tracking users' mouse movements showed that the funky warnings attracted more attention from users. The answer to dishabituation was *change*. Change the environment, change the rules, *surprise* people, and habituation will break.

SIMULATING DISASTER

Another way to trigger dishabituation is to make people experience negative outcomes. Imagine you are working furiously on your laptop when suddenly a warning message appears: "Your connection is not private. Attackers might be trying to steal your information." You ignore the message as you have done numerous times before. This time, however, is different.

Within seconds, lights start flashing on your screen, and your browser shuts down. When the chaos subsides, you restart your laptop, but something is not quite right. When you try to log on to your email account, your password does not work. You cannot get access to your bank accounts either. You heart is about to burst out of your chest. You sweat so profusely that a small puddle materializes under you. You call your bank and, to your horror, learn that your account has been drained. What is the likelihood that you will ignore online security warnings again in the future? Slim, we suspect. You have been badly burned, and as a result you will take online security much more seriously from now on.

Now, imagine that a few hours later your spouse rings. Your spouse hacked your accounts to teach you a lesson. What you went through was a "simulation." A simulation allows you to experience a disaster and to feel scared, but without in reality getting hurt. By so doing, risk habituation can break. Even though you did not experience a real cyberattack, the incident will alter your behavior.

One tool that can be used to simulate negative outcomes is virtual reality. For example, imagine construction workers experiencing a virtual accident using 3D goggles.[22] The accident might involve a plank cracking into two, causing them to fall swiftly toward the ground. The fall can feel real, triggering a strong visceral reaction. This reaction may reset risk tolerance, making people more careful on-site.

Similarly, virtual reality tools that simulate car accidents could be used to readjust the risk tolerance of experienced drivers, just as flight simulators do for pilots. Virtual reality tricks your brain to feel as if you are crashing, but without doing so in real life. It can produce dishabituation.

But this method would work only if people don't experience virtual reality accidents *repeatedly* in a short time; otherwise they might habituate, rather than dishabituate. Take, for example, an experiment that Tali conducted with her colleague Hadeel Haj Ali.[23] In the study, volunteers were invited to walk a plank suspended eighty stories high off the edge of a skyscraper. The plank was virtual, but felt very real. While the volunteers knew they were walking safely on the floor, the immersive experience tricked their brain into perceiving themselves as walking on a thin piece of wood high up in the sky. The cars and people looked small all the way down below. Planes and birds flying by seemed large. The fear was real, and walking the plank felt risky.

Some individuals refused to take even one small step on the plank. Most, however, took a step or two at first. The next time they reached the plank, they took a few more steps. The next time they reached the plank, a few more. Somewhere between the fifth and the tenth try, most people walked all the way to the edge of the plank and jumped. Over time they felt less and less anxious about walking the plank. We know this because Tali and Hadeel asked the volunteers to rate their feelings throughout the experiment and found that they became less and less anxious as time passed.

Researcher Hadeel Haj Ali walking the virtual plank in Tali's laboratory. On the right is the real world and on the left is the virtual reality Hadeel is experiencing.

So if the goal is to get people comfortable with heights, then such a virtual reality experience would be useful. But if the goal is to get people to be more cautious, you wouldn't want them to use virtual reality repeatedly, as their fear may habituate.

While we suspect that "one shot" virtual reality will be used more in the coming years to fight accidents and induce safe behavior, technology is not essential for this goal. Another way you can reset someone's risk perception is to allow them to get hurt "in real life," but just by a little. Take children, for instance. Accidents are the number one cause of death in children.[24] Some of these accidents are a product of risk habituation. Once children engage in a relatively risky behavior, such as jumping off a tall fence, without getting hurt, they can become overconfident and lose the sense of fear, which leads to greater risk-taking. But if you allow your child to suffer a minor injury, it may reduce the child's likelihood of suffering a more serious injury in the future. This is because a small negative outcome can reinstate cautious behavior.

It is not always possible to ensure that someone gets hurt "just by a little." So, another common method for dishabituation, especially in private and public institutions, is periodic training designed to alert employees to ongoing risks (for example, those associated with cybersecurity). Such training might give employees a clear and vivid sense of relevant dangers, even if they have yet to experience them directly. This can be done, for example, by sharing detailed stories of other people's accidents and mishaps. Learning of the misfortune of others will often trigger an emotional reaction.

Even with training, virtual reality, and "shaking it up," some risk habituation is likely to take place, so we need additional solutions that do not rely on individual choices alone. That is, we need architectural solutions that make activities safe, even when people are fearless or unduly complacent. Such solutions are often best. For example, the government might simply say that workers cannot be exposed to certain levels of carcinogens. People are not asked to avoid proximity to them; exposure is just banned, period.

In the same vein, you might be required to wear a motorcycle helmet or to buckle your seat belt. If so, you will be safer even if you have, over time, developed an exaggerated sense of your immunity from harm. Some of the promise of automated vehicles lies here. They do not depend on drivers' vigilance, and they should be able to avoid accidents even if drivers are overconfident or inattentive. So too, "Secure By Design" is an effort to build cybersecurity into technology products.

THE UPSIDE

From magicians to drivers, we have focused on how risk habituation results in accidents and losses. Often, though, when a psychological process seems suboptimal, deeper digging reveals that it evolved for a good reason.

Without risk habituation, we might all be an anxious bunch paralyzed by terror. Each of us has fears, some more rational than others. Maybe you are afraid of heights, flights, swimming, heartbreak, public speaking, doctor's appointments, or criticism. This is where habituation comes in handy. If you deliberately expose yourself to what scares you, your fear will slowly subside, and you will have the courage to expand your world. You may be frightened when you do something for the first time. (Do you remember learning to swim? The first time you drove on the highway? Your first kiss?) But the more you do it, the more relaxed you become. If your brain constantly responded with intense fear to stimuli that failed to harm you in the past, it would be exhausting and constraining.

Risk habituation can be crucial for human progress even when it leads to risk underestimation. Humanity needs people (entrepreneurs, astronauts, artists, athletes) who underestimate their risk, so that boundaries are expanded for all by the few who succeed—so that, in the words of the great rock climber Alex Honnold, "objectives that seemed totally crazy eventually fall within the realm of the possible."[25]

9

ENVIRONMENT:

YOU COULD LIVE NEXT TO A PIG FARM IN THE SOUTH DURING SUMMER

He can adapt to the destructive effects of our power-intoxicated technology and of our ungoverned population growth, to the dirt, pollution and noise of a New York or Tokyo. And that is the tragedy.

—RENÉ DUBOS[1]

ON A RECENT TRAIN ride to Boston from New York City, Tali was gazing out the window. Beautiful large white houses lined the tracks. She wondered whether the *clickety-clack* drove the inhabitants crazy. So Tali did what any self-respecting social scientist would do. She turned to Quora for answers.

It is both comforting and disturbing to realize that any thought generated in one's mind has been generated numerous times before in others' minds and documented for eternity on the Web. Several people have previously asked the same question as Tali, and many have shared their experiences in response. Unci

Narynin, who grew up next to a railway, says, "You will regularly hear trains coming through. I can sleep with open windows, they don't bother me. But as I have noticed with some relatives coming to visit, if they are not used to it, the trains bother them a lot and they can't find sleep."[2] Other Quora contributors who dwell near tracks agree with Narynin. They get used to the sound after some time, they say, but visitors are bothered.

"It could be worse," says Brady Wade, who resides by an airport runway. "You could live next to a pig farm in the South during summer."[3] Those living on a pig farm might beg to differ; they might be used to the *oink-oink* and the smell of pigs, but the idea of living near an airport runway might terrify them. As the comedian Robert Orben put it, "Noise pollution is a relative thing. In a city, it's a jet plane taking off. In a monastery, it's a pen that scratches."[4] And it's not just noise pollution. Air pollution, light pollution, water pollution—they are all *relative*. The extent to which they bother you depends on your past experiences. "Humans naturally adapt and we learn to live with these strains unconsciously," says Wade.[5]

This extraordinary ability helps us maintain a tolerable existence. You get used to loud noises, bad smells, dirty air, and dirty water. Yet, as we are about to see, your ability to habituate to various forms of pollution comes at a high cost.

IT'S ALL RELATIVE

Tali lived in New York City for several years, but now resides most of the year in a quiet town in Massachusetts. Because of the COVID-19 pandemic, she did not visit New York for two years. When she returned, she found the city as enticing and exciting as ever. Yet it also seemed a bit dirtier, somewhat busier, smellier. Had the city changed, or had Tali? Let's consider a study that may give us some clues.

In the early 1980s, new students to the University of California at Los Angeles (UCLA) were invited to participate in a study on migration.[6] Los Angeles has the dubious honor of ranking number one on the list of cities with the worst air quality in the United States.*[7] Within the developed Western world, Los Angeles is ranked as one of the worst (closely followed by New York City). What's more, the UCLA campus is located smack in the middle of an especially high-smog area. The new students had all moved to campus three weeks before. Some had relocated from other neighborhoods within the city, while others had come from different cities, including Honolulu and Portland, that have low levels of air pollution.

Suzanne and Daryl were two of the freshmen who volunteered for the study. Daryl grew up in downtown Los Angeles and Suzanne in Cheyenne, Wyoming, which is among the cleanest cities in the United States for air pollution. When they arrived at the lab, they were shown photos of outdoor scenes, such as a city skyline or a valley with a foothill. Half the photos had some smog and half did not; the amount of smog, when present, varied from a lot to a little. For each photo, Suzanne and Daryl had to judge whether smog was present. Suzanne was

---

* We note that different lists provide slightly different rankings.

much more likely to report the presence of smog in the photos than Daryl. Daryl reported smog in photos only when the levels were quite high. The levels of smog Suzanne and Daryl perceived were a function of what they had habituated to.

It was not just Suzanne and Daryl; those arriving at UCLA from clean areas were more likely to notice air pollution. This means that you perceive your surroundings not according to some objective criterion of the number of particulates in the air, but according to a subjective criterion that is contingent on what is familiar to you. These criteria are different depending on whether you live in London or Moscow, in Copenhagen or Beijing, in New York City or a Massachusetts suburb, in Los Angeles or Honolulu, or in Berlin or Rome.

Imagine that you were born in a city full of smog and had never left town. You would consider smog normal. You would likely detect pollution only when the air had more smog than the baseline to which you had become habituated. But if you lived in a clean-air region most of your life, you would be used to blue skies, and as a result even a bit of smog would stand out. It might be startling. This is why people are often unaware that they are living in highly polluted environments. In the United Kingdom, for example, only 10 percent of the population rated their air quality as poor, even though air pollution breaches legal limits in 88 percent of UK regions.[8]

It follows that if you have been living in a high-smog area for a while and are no longer able to detect smog, you will not consider smog a problem. This is exactly what the researchers found. When asked to list the community problems on campus, newcomers to Los Angeles such as Suzanne were more likely to mention smog than long-termers such as Daryl. Students such as Suzanne from Wyoming, Ethel from Hawaii, and Larry from Oregon were more likely to mention respiratory problems than long-termers such as Daryl from downtown Los Angeles or Harriet from North Hollywood. Daryl and Harriet believed their health was less vulnerable to smog than that of the newcomers.[9]

Are Daryl and Harriet right? Are they physically less vulnerable to smog because they grew up in a smog-filled city?

There could be a pinch of truth in their statements; some studies show that your body can physically change to adjust to pollution. Physiologically, you may become less reactive to potentially harmful pollutants if you have been exposed to them for a while.[10] But it is also likely that Daryl and Harriet are seeing the glass half-full. Most people view their world through rose-colored glasses (one of us wrote a book about this). We tend to believe that we are a bit smarter than average, more interesting, and more fun.[11] We think that we are less likely to get COVID[12] than the other guy, less likely to be in a car accident, and more likely to get a promotion. We think that our health care system is better than the one in the nearby city. On climate change, many of us see the overall dangers, but believe our own town will be just fine.[13]

Some of this is a form of denial; some of it involves focusing on the silver lining and rationalization. Because Daryl and Harriet have spent their whole lives in a polluted city, they are more motivated to believe they are especially resistant to smog. Viewing smog and noise as harmless, and themselves as immune, can help Daryl and Harriet reduce stress and anxiety.

In theory, Suzanne, who moved to LA from fresh-aired Wyoming, may at first be unhappy due to the pollution, but she should become happier as she habituates to it. Puzzlingly, however, it is hard to see such a trend in the existing data. That is, people do not necessarily become happier after living in a polluted area for a while relative to when they first arrived.[14]

We asked Christopher Barrington-Leigh, an associate professor at the Institute for Health and Social Policy at McGill University, why this is so. Chris responded, "How to separate other location-fixed effects from the location pollution to which you'd be interested in accommodation? Sounds hard!"

Let us translate. Chris is saying that many different factors affect people's happiness as they move from one place to another and adapt. Many of them have nothing at all to do with pollution. (Do they have friends? A good parking place? A good job?) Some factors are highly correlated with pollution. For example, polluted areas may have more traffic, which means longer commute times. Polluted areas may have more people, which means more social opportunities. All these factors can affect your happiness in different directions, and it is nearly impossible to account for them all to pinpoint the impact of pollution itself on happiness as people get used to a new environment.

So while some work has been done on air pollution and happiness, it leaves important questions unanswered. The work does tend to suggest that people in Honolulu (or Portland or any other clean city) are not *necessarily* happier than people in LA (or NYC or any other polluted city). But the research shows that on days *when pollution is worse than the local seasonal average*, people tend to be less happy than otherwise.[15] Short-term changes in pollution decrease happiness. This is strong evidence of habituation. That is, if you are used to clear air and suddenly experience a day with high smog, perhaps due to strong winds, your well-being on that day will be lower than otherwise. But if every day has high smog, your well-being might not be much affected by it.

0.7 BATHS PER DAY

A somewhat cleaner picture (no pun intended) emerges in carefully controlled experiments. Laboratory experiments enable you to control for many factors, which is difficult to do with surveys. Consider a study conducted in Denmark in the early 1990s. Two scientists, Lars Gunnarsen and Ole Fanger, invited a group of Danish volunteers to the climate chambers of the Laboratory of Heating and Air-Conditioning.[16] Because the chambers are highly regulated, Lars and Ole could fully control and measure the composition of the air.

At first, Lars and Ole asked groups of eight volunteers to enter a closed chamber. The pollution the researchers were about to test was created by the volunteers themselves. Don't get us wrong; the volunteers were a clean bunch. They reported changing their underwear every day and on average took 0.7 baths every twenty-four hours. Nevertheless, each emitted odors that polluted the air.

Lars and Ole found that upon entering the chamber, people reported the intensity of the odor as much higher than they did eight minutes later. Two minutes after that, they said there was only a slight odor, which was certainly acceptable.

Lars and Ole found a similar pattern when they asked volunteers to enter a room filled with tobacco smoke. If you are old enough, you may remember the experience of entering a smoked-filled club (this was before no-smoking legislation); the smell of cigarettes filled your lungs as you attempted to part your way through the smoky air. You may even remember the days when commercial planes were a tobacco fest. Miraculously, no more than twenty minutes would go by before most people forgot all about the heavy smoke—only to be reminded of it the next day when the scent made its way from the previous night's clothing into their nostrils.[17]

The Danish scientists concluded that habituation to pollution may be one reason that there are relatively few complaints about enclosed areas with bad air. As long as the odors are relatively constant—that is, the levels of smoke or bodily odors do not abruptly alter—people habituate within a short time.

To make people care about poor air quality, whether it is indoors or outdoors, dishabituation is needed. If people dishabituate to smoke or smog, they will be more likely to call for better conditions. Consider the use of "clean air chambers," which would create temporary dishabituation to pollution. The idea is to set up small spaces in which air quality is high, where individuals can rest for short periods. Once people step out of the clean air chamber and back on the street, they will be more likely to notice pollution.

You may wonder why humans have evolved a brain that

causes us to stop perceiving odors, smog, or smoke after a short habituation period. To answer this question, consider sound editing. When a technician records a segment, let's say an interview for a documentary, she makes sure to record a few seconds of "quiet time." This recording provides background noise (such as the sound of the air-conditioning and traffic) so that later she can subtract that sound to make the important bits (such as conversation) stand out. Our brain edits input like a professional sound technician. It filters out noise, smells, and other "background" stimuli so that new and potentially significant stimuli can easily be detected. This can be important for survival.

Consider a dog that has been lying for hours in a rose-filled garden. The dog's olfactory neurons ceased responding to the constant smell of roses a while ago, which makes it much easier for the dog to detect the faint scent of the coyote that is quickly approaching.[18] This is all well and good. The problem emerges when the brain filters out some "background stimulus" that is not innocuous, but is killing us very, very, very slowly.

A FROG WILL JUMP *IF IT CAN*

It all began in 1869 when Friedrich Goltz, a German physiologist, set out to find the physical location of the soul. He suspected it resided in the brain. To test his hypothesis, he conducted an experiment with two frogs. One frog was healthy, intact, and slimy. The other was also slimy, but had had its brain removed. Goltz placed them both in a large pot of water, which he then raised to a boil slowly.[19] Guess what happened next?

Indeed, the frog without a brain remained in the pot. A frog without a nervous system cannot jump. The intact frog escaped the pot with an impressive hop when the water reached 25°C (77°F).

Yet, a few years later, two additional studies, conducted by scientists named Heinzmann and Fratscher, found conflicting results—namely, that perfectly intact frogs did not try to escape a pot of boiling water as long as it was heated gradually.[20] The frogs soaked obliviously in the water unaware that the temperature was gradually rising until it was too late.

Why these two scientists observed different results from Goltz is unclear. Regardless, the boiling frog quickly became a metaphor for the danger of detrimental changes that happen slowly, with climate change being a prominent example.

When yet more studies were conducted, Goltz was found to be right after all. The frog *will* change location when the water reaches a certain temperature regardless of how gradual the increase is.[21] This led to a passionate debate about whether it was, or was not, acceptable to use the boiling-frog tale as an analogy to the human condition. Nobel Prize winners[22] and *New York Times* bestselling authors[23] have expressed strong opinions on the matter. Some say no, it is inappropriate to use this analogy, given that we know that the frog will jump out of the water (assuming it has an intact brain). Others say it is fine to use the analogy if it is clearly stated that scientific evidence shows that the frog will escape the pot in time.[24]

We suggest a new twist to the boiling-frog tale, which might be acceptable to all. The frog is placed in a pot of water that is heated gradually. Sophisticated creature that it is, the frog jumps out of the water before it boils to death, only to discover that the pot is floating on a large body of water that is itself coming to a boil very, very slowly. There is nowhere to go!

WARM, WARMER, HOT, HOTTER, BURNING

Amphibians aside, will *Homo sapiens* float calmly in a hot pot as long as the temperature rises slowly, or will people scream and shout? A group of scientists from MIT, UC Davis, Vancouver, and Boulder turned to Twitter for answers.[25] They wondered whether people would notice disturbing weather trends when they occurred gradually. If people are inclined to twist and shout, surely Twitter would be the place they would go to do so.

Imagine you live in London and experience a day when the temperature is pretty warm, say 32°C (~90°F). You can bet that everyone will be commenting on the weather. In contrast, if you were in Dubai, no one would mention a 32°C day, though a snow flurry would certainly cause a buzz. People notice and talk about the weather if it stands out relative to what they are used to—if it is surprising.

Now imagine that Dubai experienced a snow flurry every year for the past ten years. When a flurry falls again, would you bother to mention it to your friends and family? What if you lived in London and encountered a 32°C day, which was preceded by a 31°C day, which was preceded by a 30°C day, which was preceded by a 29°C day—would you mention the hot weather to your colleagues?

A group of scientists, headed by Frances Moore, eavesdropped on people's conversations on Twitter to find out; between 2014 and 2016 they measured the weekly volume of weather-related tweets. They found that people did indeed tweet more about the weather if it was unusual for the relevant time and place. That is, if the humidity was high in Maine, you would see lots of weather-related tweets in Maine, but that same level of humidity experienced in Florida would not trigger a Twitter storm because the weather in Florida is often humid. In an area that had been experiencing warmer weather than baseline for a while, fewer weather-related tweets appeared on hot than cold days. And in an area that had been experiencing colder weather than baseline for a while, fewer weather-related tweets appeared on cold than hot days.

On average it took between two to eight years for people to stop thinking that extreme temperatures were unusual. This happened because people adjusted their perception of "normal." Eventually extreme weather was perceived as just another day on earth.

Frances and her team believe their data indicated a "boiling frog" effect and warn that "the negative effects of a gradually changing environment become normalized so that corrective measures are never adopted."[26] Habituation creates an obstacle, because if people do not perceive the change, they will not recognize the problem. Without such recognition, the work of climate activists becomes even harder.

A question remains: Do we fail to *feel* very hot or very cold weather if it changes gradually, or do we just fail to tweet about it? Do we emotionally and physically habituate to weather changes? Frances and her team did not find evidence for that in their data. However, studies in which body temperature is carefully manipulated, and physiological response measured, suggest the answer is yes.

LESS SHIVERING

In March 1961 a group of army men from Fort Knox, Kentucky, participated in an unusual and somewhat unpleasant experiment.[27] The men were stripped down and then spent eight hours a day for thirty-one days in a temperature-controlled room. The temperature was set to exactly 53.24°F (11.8°C). Normal room temperature is between 68°F (20°C) and 77°F (25°C). Each day their physiological reactions were measured. It transpired that the nude men shivered less and less with each passing day.

Shivering is a response to the stress induced by cold; it produces heat due to muscle movements. Despite the reduction in shivering, the men's rectal temperatures (we told you this experiment was unpleasant) remained constant. This means that the soldiers' bodies had acclimatized to the cold temperature—they produced sufficient heat without shivering.

You may wonder if the soldiers were especially likely to habituate to the cold due to their army training. But the Fort Knox men were no anomaly. The same phenomenon was observed in civilians. In 2014, for example, another group of men spent three hours a day in a bath of 57°F (14°C) water for twenty days.[28] We have no idea what they did in the bath for so many hours every day. Regardless, once again a gradual reduction of shivering was observed over time. The men also reported less and less discomfort, and their blood work showed they were experiencing reduced stress as the days passed. They were habituating.

We are all capable of habituating physiologically to otherwise uncomfortable weather, but many of us do not allow this natural process to take place. We fight the cold with cups of warm herbal tea and chicken soup; we put on mittens, a woolly hat and scarf, and make a nice warm fire. Similarly, we fight the heat with air-conditioning, cold showers, and iced tea. Strictly speaking, changing our behavior such that we are less bothered by the heat and cold is a form of adaptation, but it prevents the physiological kind. To get used to the freezing cold or steaming heat, we need to abandon parkas and fans and expose ourselves to discomfort a few times a day. If we do so, within a couple of weeks our body will start changing and we will feel less cold or less hot.[29]

To be sure, there are limits to our ability to habituate and adapt. Exposure to extreme temperatures will eventually kill you. But within a reasonable range, habituation can be quick and effective. Just think about the last time you jumped into a cold pool or entered a steaming sauna. In the first few seconds, the sensation is intense, but it then subsides rapidly, sometimes fading completely.

The combination of behavioral adaptation (turning on the AC or heating, taking ice baths, putting on a sweatshirt, installing double-glazed windows), normalization of extreme conditions (the tendency to perceive extreme weather, smog, and constant noise as normal as they become frequent), and physiological habituation (our body's natural tendency to adjust to the environment) all allow us to function in heat, cold, smog, and noise, but at a likely cost. Habituation and adaptation will keep us floating happily in the warming pot, but not forever. The environmentalist René Dubos[30] believed that habituation and adaptation would enable us to survive the ecological crisis but eventually destroy the quality of human life. Some are even less optimistic.

IFR, NOT VFR

The debates over air pollution in general and climate change in particular are complex, and obviously many political and economic factors sway people's views. What is less obvious is that because of habituation, significant changes in air quality and to the climate will go unnoticed.

People notice rapid changes: flooding, wildfires, extreme heat, and drought are not exactly invisible. But when changes in temperature and weather occur gradually, we may not perceive them. Some of the changes that we do not notice now may eventually have serious negative effects on our lives. The changes increase the risks of exceedingly harmful events that we might not be able to address until it is too late. It should, however, be easier to see the problem by *measuring what we can measure*: emissions of greenhouse gases, and also of standard air pollutants, such as particulate matter, ozone, nitrogen oxide, lead, and sulfur dioxide.

For many environmental problems, habituation ensures that our sensations and feelings will not be an adequate guide to what is good or bad, safe or dangerous, and so we need to find ways to evaluate risks objectively. We need to switch from using Visual Flight Rules (VFR) to using Instrumental Flight Rules (IFR).

When pilots fly in good visibility and clear skies, they can rely on their eyes and brain to assess where they are and what they need to do to land safely at their destination. But using your senses as a guide when flying a plane is safe only when you have information outside your window to enable your brain to figure out where you are and how to get to where you are going. If the necessary information is obstructed by clouds, rain, and so forth, you must rely on technology.

Your instruments will indicate your exact location, speed, and angle. Sometimes that information even contradicts your sensations, as in the case of vertigo, when pilots feel that they are ascending toward the sky while the instruments indicate they are rapidly descending toward the ground. Ignoring the instruments and relying on perception has led to multiple aircraft disasters and a number of deaths.

We are now entering an IFR period. We cannot rely purely on our vision, tactile sensations, emotions, and memory to assess changes to the environment. We need to turn to science and technology to provide us with accurate information (such as temperature changes over time) and use the data to guide our actions. IFR, not VFR.

PART IV

SOCIETY

10

PROGRESS:

BREAKING THE CHAINS OF
LOW EXPECTATIONS

We must learn how to be surprised.
Not to adjust ourselves.

—ABRAHAM JOSHUA HESCHEL[1]

I N THE EARLY 1950S a small child named Jorge Bucay went to
the circus in his hometown of Buenos Aires.[2] The show was
spectacular: trapeze artists, clowns, jugglers, magicians. There
were daring feats of courage and breathtaking beauty. And
then there were the animals!

Because of concerns about animal welfare, circus animals
are now rare, but back in the 1950s they were everywhere.
Monkeys, parrots, and, of course, elephants. The animals were
trained to play musical instruments, ride a bicycle, and dance.
The gigantic elephants were often the children's favorite.

Jorge too loved the elephants. After the end of the performance, Jorge noticed something mysterious on his way out:

the large elephant was chained by the foot to a small stake in the ground. Young Jorge found this baffling. The stake was just a tiny piece of wood, and the elephant was so big and strong. Surely the elephant could easily free itself and flee? Why didn't it do so?

None of the adults seemed to know. The question stayed with Jorge until fifty years later, when he finally met a knowledgeable man with an answer. When the elephant was just a baby, the man explained, it had been attached to a tiny pole that was partially driven into the ground. The little elephant tried desperately to set itself free, but small as it was, it could not. It tried and tried again. But after a while, the little elephant simply accepted its fate. As the elephant grew, it gained enormous strength; it could uproot mature trees and lift heavy stones. It could easily have escaped, but it never tried.

Perhaps it did not occur to the elephant that it now could, or that a different life was possible. The constraint was no longer in the elephant's muscles. It was in its mind.

The elephant seemed to have habituated to the limitations on its movements at a young age and stopped rebelling against them. Maybe it no longer considered the limitations to be limitations. Perhaps the elephant eventually perceived its limited range of movement in the same way that human beings think about their inability to fly like birds—just a matter of fact. So the elephant was less angry, less frightened, and less sad. But still, it was trapped.

WOMEN IN CHAINS

In the United States prior to 1974 it was perfectly legal, as a matter of federal law, to deny a woman a credit card based on her gender. Before 1968, it was legal to deny a woman housing because she was a woman. Before 1964, it was legal to deny a woman a job based on her sex. In many states, it was legal to exclude women from juries. Women did not have equal rights; many found it difficult to obtain higher education and secure interesting jobs, and when they did, they were not paid as much as men. Women were doing most of the household chores and childcare (as they still do). Yet, the data shows that in the 1950s and 1960s women were not less happy than men. When women were asked how happy they were on a scale ranging from "very happy" to "not too happy," their ratings were equal to those of men, and some studies suggest that women were even happier than men.[3] They also seemed to have as much self-esteem as men. How could that be?

For thousands of years, women lacked rights that men had and were subject to pervasive discrimination. Women could not vote; they could not own property; in many cases they could not choose whom to marry. They were chained. While some women fought these chains and made important progress, the overwhelming majority accepted life as it was. Habituation did its thing, and like the elephant, most women did not rebel. We suspect that many were partially blind to those chains, perhaps not realizing that a different life could be possible. Others accepted them. Low expectations meant that women were not surprised when they were denied education, jobs, and property ownership.

Eventually, however, the group of women who did attempt to cut the chains grew and strengthened. With the help of the women's rights movement, large gains were made in the 1970s, 1980s, 1990s, and onward. In many nations, antidiscrimination laws were introduced, and many more women obtained higher education and participated in the job market. But as the chains became weaker, something unexpected happened. Women did not become happier. In fact, their happiness declined to such an extent that on many measures men were now happier than women. This pattern was observed not only in the United States but also in Belgium, Denmark, France, Great Britain, Greece, Ireland, Italy, Luxembourg, the Netherlands, Portugal, and Spain, among others.[4]

This does not mean that inequality and discrimination are good things. Not at all. But it raises some serious puzzles.

If you look at women's self-reported well-being across countries, you find that as societal conditions for women become better, women often report *lower* life satisfaction. Women seem to report that they are happier in countries where inequality is greater.[5] Let's consider why.

Today, in many Western nations, women are told they have rights equivalent to those of men—to be an astronaut, an investment banker, a judge, and even a prime minister or president. Women have the legal right to be paid as much as men, so they compare their achievements to those of their male counterparts. But guess what?

In reality, opportunities are not close to equal. Women have legal rights in many countries, even equal rights, yes, but much of the time, discrimination continues in multiple forms.

Women are told that household chores should be equally divided between partners. Yet women around the world continue to do the laundry, the shopping, the childcare, the cleaning, the cooking, the form filling, the homework helping. They do that even in cases when their jobs are more demanding than those of their male partners. Even when the wives are the sole breadwinner in the family, they still spend the same amount of time on household chores as their unemployed husbands. Those women do not only earn the bread, they also slice it up and make the children's lunch sandwiches too.[6]

In contrast, in the 1950s in the United States (and other countries) while women also did the majority of household chores, many did not have the highest aspirations or the greatest expectations, at least for those things that were unavailable to them. They habituated to existing social norms. By contrast, women in modern Western societies expect equality. Yet, daily, that expectation is not fulfilled.

This gap between what you expect (equal pay, equal opportunity, respect) and what you get (less pay, limited opportunity, disrespect) creates unhappiness. Neuroscientists call this gap between expectations and outcomes a *negative prediction error*. As we will soon see, while these prediction errors induce unhappiness in the short term, they are critical for progress.

SURPRISE!

You may not be aware of it, but at this very moment your brain is trying to predict what will come next. What will be the next word in this . . . (yes) sentence; how will the page of this book feel against your hand when you turn the page; how will the coffee taste as you move the hot mug toward your lips. If you make good predictions, you will not be surprised by the temperature of the liquid or the next word you read.

You also make longer-term predictions. "I will get the assistant manager job at the bank," "Georgina is going to leave me," "It is going to be freezing up on the ski slope." The reason almost every neuron in your brain is engaged in some sort of prediction is obvious—by predicting what will come next you will be better prepared. If you are well prepared, you will avoid freezing on the slope or losing your house to Georgina.

But sometimes you are wrong. Surprise! You didn't get the job at the bank. Surprise! Georgina stays with you forever.

These mistakes (or prediction errors) are important—they are "teaching signals" from which you can learn about the world around you and correct your expectations. Some of the mistakes are wonderful ("Georgina stayed!") and some are not so wonderful ("Didn't get the job!"). Your brain must have a clear signal that indicates whether the surprise is good or bad. This is because if the surprise is good, you should continue doing what you were doing (be nice to Georgina and tell her you love her), but if the surprise is bad, you need to change something (edit your CV, get more experience). So, while some neurons in your brain simply signal "Surprise!," others code for two types of surprises—good and bad. Perhaps the most "famous" are the dopaminergic neurons.

Dopaminergic neurons synthesize the neurotransmitter dopamine. A neurotransmitter is a chemical that is released by one neuron to another neuron as a way of communicating a message. Dopaminergic neurons are constantly firing. Even when nothing much is going on, they are firing. But when something is surprising in a good way ("She loves me!"), they fire even more, signaling to the rest of the brain that what just happened is better than expected. When something is surprising in a bad way ("No job offer!"), they quiet down.

This unusual quietness delivers a message to the rest of the brain: What just happened is worse than we expected. The first signal is called a *positive prediction error* and the second a *negative prediction error.* Prediction errors are closely associated with your mood. When positive prediction errors are triggered, you feel great, and when negative prediction errors are triggered, you feel bad.[7]

Broadly speaking, women in the 1950s may have had fewer negative prediction errors than women in the 1980s because women in the 1950s had low expectations and were less likely to be negatively surprised. The same logic follows for a range of scenarios. When people adapt their expectations downward, terrible conditions (such as corruption, poor health, or being tied to a stick) do not affect their happiness as much as they would otherwise.[8] Low expectations mean no negative prediction errors, which means that bad conditions daily may go unnoticed.

LOW EXPECTATIONS

People's preferences adapt to what is available. Social theorists Jon Elster[9] and Amartya Sen[10] refer to this as the problem of "adaptive preferences": if you cannot have something, you might end up not wanting it at all. Empirical evidence supports the claim that people adapt to deprivation. In countries where people have less freedom, freedom matters *less* to people's well-being because they don't expect to have it.[11] They may have less autonomy, but because of habituation they might be able to maintain a reasonable level of welfare. Income affects happiness the least in Africa, which is also the poorest continent on earth, partly because in Africa citizens have lower expectations.[12] In Afghanistan, where crime and corruption are among the highest in the world, crime and corruption affect people's well-being the least.[13]

To be clear, people in Afghanistan are not joyous. Poverty, insecurity, and political instability have taken their toll. The country ranks at the bottom of the world's list in happiness.[14] Yet if you moved to Afghanistan tomorrow morning, we suspect that you would be much less happy than the average citizen there. Afghan citizens have, to some extent, habituated to their circumstances and hold low expectations, just as the circus elephant adapted to his. You, by contrast, have likely grown accustomed to running water, sufficient food, and a sense of security. The lack of any of these will produce a negative prediction error, one that will likely shake you to the core.

You may be thinking, "Okay, great, let's just all lower our expectations and live happily ever after." It's hardly that simple. Low expectations can lead to a big problem: you might stop fighting the suboptimal conditions (or perhaps never even begin). In Elster's words, "adaptive preferences have both a numbing effect and a paralyzing effect: they alleviate the pain while also blunting any urge to act."[15]

You might stay in a relationship or a job that is less than ideal or not try to alter it for the better. You may accept your weak muscles instead of hitting the gym or habituate to constant back pain instead of seeing a doctor. Data shows that the demand for better health care is often *lower* in societies that need improvement the most compared to those that have excellent care.[16] This is because people in nations with less than wonderful health care systems habituate; they expect less, so they might be satisfied, or not be horribly dissatisfied, with a system that would frustrate and shock people in other nations.

So while unmet expectations cause unhappiness, unhappiness might be necessary for change. And once change happens, happiness can be regained. Let's take gender inequality as an example. At first, improving opportunities and expectations for women lowered female happiness, but once conditions improved beyond a certain point, they were associated with happiness gains.[17] The relationship between women's freedom and well-being is U-shaped. Initial gains in women's rights appeared to produce reductions in self-esteem and happiness because expectations were mismatched with reality. Yet, as women's social conditions continued to improve, and reality started to catch up with expectations, well-being increased.

In no place on earth do women have opportunities equal to men's. We do not know if in such a society women will be as happy with their lives as men are. We may not live to see such a society ourselves (thousands of years of oppression take a while to reverse), but we like to think that if and when it does happen, the happiness gap will disappear.

BREAKING THE CHAINS

The obvious conundrum is that no movement aimed at breaking chains could ever occur if habituation were universal and complete. If it were, the conditions would be settled for all time. One of George Orwell's characters put it chillingly in *1984*: "If you want a picture of the future, imagine a boot stamping on a human face—forever."[18]

For social movements to arise, there must be someone who does not entirely habituate—who is uncomfortable with some practice, or some situation, and who is willing to say or do something about it.

Here is a highly stylized account of what sometimes happens. Society consists of a range of people, who are highly diverse in their attitudes. Some people will have habituated entirely to what exists, including injustice; they will take current practices as background noise, or as a normal and natural part of life. Other people will have habituated a lot; they will hear a voice of protest in their heads, but that voice is relatively quiet. Some people will have habituated only a little; at some level they will be outraged or appalled, but they will be keenly aware that change is difficult or unlikely, which means that they will silence themselves.

What is the point—they might think—of beating one's head against the wall? These people engage in *preference falsification*; because of existing norms, they do not reveal what they actually prefer and think. They might be willing to do that, but only if norms start to shift.

In this stylized account, people also have diverse thresholds for action. Those who have habituated least will be entirely willing to act, even if they stand alone. We can call them the zeros. Other people, who have habituated a little, will be willing to act, but not to go first; they need someone to follow. They are the ones. Other people will be willing to act but will not go first or second; they need precursors. They are the twos. The twos are followed by the threes, and the threes by the fours, and the fours by the fives, all the way up to the infinites (understood as people who have fully habituated and will not rebel under any circumstances).

In this account, change will arise only after the right kinds of social interactions. If the ones see the zeros, the ones will move; if the twos see the ones and the zeros, the twos will move; if the threes see the twos and the ones, the threes will move too. We will eventually witness some kind of social cascade, in which a large-scale movement takes hold.

But a mystery remains: How can we explain the people who do not habituate—the zeros? We do not have a full answer to that question, but we think that part of it lies in their likely exposure, at some stage, to something *dis*habituating—something that made existing practices no longer seem natural and inevitable, and that delivered a kind of jolt or a surprise. That something might be a different practice in some other time or place; it might be an exercise of imagination, prompted by some encounter or experience. We call these people *dishabituation entrepreneurs*, and we will have a lot more to say about them in the next chapter.

We also believe that knowledge about habituation can produce dishabituation entrepreneurs. That is, after learning about all the ways people habituate, you may be able to detect and focus on the suboptimal aspects of your life to which you have become accustomed. You may notice those less fortunate features of your home life and work life, and of society, that you have overlooked. Granted, in many situations you are better off accepting things that are not perfect or even not at all great. The hope, though, is that awareness of all the ways our brains blind us to the constant and expected will help you distinguish the "chains" you should accept from those you should try to break.

11

DISCRIMINATION:

THE GENTLE JEW, THE MINISKIRT-WEARING SCIENTIST, AND THE CHILDREN WHO WERE JUST NOT COOL

We shall remain prisoners of culture
unless we become aware of the process and
force ourselves to confront it.

—JOHN HOWARD GRIFFIN[1]

IN THE SUMMER OF 2016, Margaret Sawyer, a former executive of a not for profit, visited a pool in Salida, Colorado, with her kids. She noticed a Red Cross poster pinned to a billboard.[2] Take a close look at the poster on the next page.

Does anything about the poster strike you as odd?

Not long ago, Cass was in a group of about twenty people who were shown the poster and asked that question. Most people in the group did not notice much. But a Black person in

Cass's group immediately saw something: The "Not Cool" label is associated almost entirely with children of color. After the group's attention was drawn to the association, everyone in the group saw it—and they were amazed that they had not seen it before. Once it was pointed out, people could not *not* see it.

When the Red Cross initially released the poster, no one in the organization detected the problem (or at least none spoke up if they did). The poster was posted on billboards of numerous pools and no one complained.

Until Margaret Sawyer came along.

When she first noticed it in the Salida pool, she assumed that it was an anomaly—a vintage poster. But that same weekend she saw the same poster in a pool in Fort Morgan, Colorado. She realized it was not a 1970s poster—it was part of a recent campaign. She took a photo of it and posted it on her Twitter account. At first, many users did not see anything wrong. "I don't get it. What is racist about this pic?" one comment read. Once Margaret pointed out the problem, however, a public outcry followed. The media picked up the story, and the Red Cross apologized for "this inadvertent action."[3]

The key word here is *inadvertent*. The Red Cross did not mean to release a racist ad. Rather, the people of the Red Cross were not aware it was one. Pool workers across the country, who pinned the poster to bulletin boards, did not notice it either. Neither did thousands of poolgoers and numerous Twitter users. But one person—Margaret Sawyer—changed all that. She was person zero.

In a world where bias and discrimination are the norm, most people become habituated to them. We do not *perceive* the discrimination around us because we expect it. One more time: we notice what is surprising and different, but gloss over what is the same and anticipated. And here the problem lies: we cannot work to change what we do not perceive. Until someone comes along and makes what is in front of us clear and salient.

THE GENTLE JEW

A few decades ago, Cass was invited to go to South Africa, to advise some members of the all-white apartheid government about a possible constitution for a postapartheid nation. Cass had some trepidation about accepting the invitation, but before doing so, he was assured that those who were involved were strongly in favor of racial equality, and that they hoped to help design a constitution that would eliminate the legacy of apartheid. During his visit, Cass got along particularly well with one of the South African judges, a leader of the effort, who was sharp, learned, and amiable. Cass liked the judge, and the judge seemed to like him.

At the final dinner, and after a few drinks, the judge repeated Cass's last name about six times, with what seemed to be mild displeasure and perhaps a little confusion: "Sunstein, Sunstein, Sunstein, Sunstein, Sunstein, Sunstein." Cass thought that was peculiar and perhaps not entirely friendly. What was so interesting about his last name? He looked at the judge quizzically.

The judge paused and then said, "We have a Jew on our court. We call him the Gentle Jew."

Cass was startled by this statement. The judge meant to be amusing; he had no idea that his utterance might seem odd or inappropriate. Looking around the table, Cass immediately noticed that no one else at the dinner seemed to take note of the incident, or even to think that there had been an incident. Cass was quite certain that this type of behavior would have caused a reaction in his own country. But what is unusual and attention-grabbing in one culture is often unnoticeable in another.

Norms change across time and place. Certain acts and comments will stand out in one culture or decade, but not in another. We habituate to the norms that we live with. Transporting ourselves from one place to another, or from one decade to another (for example, when watching old films), enables

us to see what others in that place and period do not. For example, smoking is fine and cool in some times and places, and
even romantic, but in other times and places, it signals that
you do not care about yourself or others. People get habituated
to the presence of smokers, and then they get dishabituated.

In some countries the word *homo* is commonly used to describe a gay person. People in those countries do not pause
when they hear it or use it, and most are completely unaware
that in other places it is considered a slur and rarely used. If a
citizen of the latter country travels to the former and hears the
slur, the person will be jarred and probably respond negatively.

Whether we will, or will not, perceive something to be dis-
criminatory depends on what we are used to in our environment, but it may also depend on which side of the fence we
are on—one group or another. About ten years ago Tali was at
a science meeting with about a dozen people. A male professor was chairing the meeting. He turned to a female student
and mentioned that he had heard through the grapevine that
she had received an invitation to give a talk considered prestigious. He asked, "Did they invite you so you could parade in
a miniskirt onstage?" The comment was made loud and clear,
yet it did not seem that anyone took note. The meeting continued as usual.

Not so long ago, such comments were not altogether unusual. Male professors would often comment on the appearance of women scientists. One woman, an invited speaker,
was labeled "rather large" and another "quite hot." "How are
you able to sit beside her and concentrate?" a professor once
asked a male student, referring to the student's female mentor.

Later Tali emailed the professor from the science meeting, who immediately issued an apology—in retrospect he could see the problem. Tali also asked her colleagues who were in attendance, almost all men, about the incident. Some did not notice it; others did not think it was of much importance. Such comments occurred daily and so it was nothing unusual. The one other person who did take offense was a female colleague. Which leads us to an interesting question—do those who are subjected to bias habituate to it less? To what extent are they more likely to perceive it?

IN ANOTHER'S SHOES

When we experience discrimination repeatedly, we learn to expect it to some degree, at least in its less egregious forms. We habituate, just as the elephant did to its chains, and women prior to the 1970s did to their positions. We are thus less likely to respond than if discrimination were unusual. Nevertheless, when you are on the receiving end of bias, you may habituate more slowly and perhaps not perfectly. In *Chariots of Fire*, the celebrated film about British Olympians from the 1920s, Harold Abrahams, the Jewish sprinter, captures the feeling well:

> It's an ache, a helplessness, an anger. One feels humiliated. Sometimes I say to myself, "Hey, steady on, you're imagining all this." And then I catch that look again. Catch it on the edge of a remark, feel a cold reluctance in a handshake.[4]

Why are victims of discrimination less likely to habituate than onlookers? One reason, we suspect, is that even when discrimination is frequent, it contrasts with the image one has of oneself. A female pilot may, to some degree, get used to the possibility that others believe that she is less qualified than most men, which may lower her confidence somewhat. Yet such attitudes will still contrast with her daily experience of skillfully controlling an aircraft. This mismatch—between what we observe our abilities to be, and the group-based expectations of us—will lead to constant "error signals" in our brain, which will reduce the rate of habituation.

It follows that if you transform yourself from male to female, white to Black, or straight to gay, you will be more likely to perceive discrimination that you would otherwise not see. This is exactly what is reported by people who have undergone such changes.

Here is a famous and influential example—a tale of habituation and dishabituation. In 1959 the journalist John Howard Griffin had his skin temporarily darkened, so that he could pass as Black. For weeks, he traveled in the American South, visiting Georgia, Mississippi, Louisiana, Alabama, and Arkansas. Griffin's motivation was simple: "If we could only put ourselves in the shoes of others to see how we would react, then we might become aware of the injustice of discrimination and the tragic inhumanity of every kind of prejudice." His 1961 book, *Black Like Me*, was a sensation.[5]

We acknowledge that many people are now offended by the book, not because of its vivid portrayal of racism (which made it controversial at the time), but because of what they consider to be its presumptuousness. What we want to emphasize is that when it was published, it gave white people a sense of what it would be like to be a Black person in the South—to visit a kind of upside-down world in which one would be treated with rage, brutality, suspicion, or contempt, despite being quiet, honest, and kind.

Griffin described a world where you could be threatened or dismissed for no reason. "Nothing can describe the withering horror of this. You feel lost, sick at heart before such unmasked hatred, not so much because it threatens you as because it shows humans in such an inhuman light. You see a kind of insanity, something so obscene the very obscenity of it (rather than its threat) terrifies you."[6]

Griffin says that his experience helped him to see that "culture—learned behavior patterns so ingrained that they produce involuntary reactions—is a prison." He learned to live with constant fear.[7]

Something akin to Griffin's experience is shared by individuals who have changed their gender. Transgender scientists, for example, report a significant and surprising change in their colleagues' attitudes toward them following their transition. Once in the other gender's shoes, they see things they were not able to see before.

It seems, then, that one way we can dishabituate is by temporarily putting ourselves in another's skin. Doing what Griffin did at scale is impractical, but modern technology allows us to take tiny steps in different shoes, using virtual reality. Do you want to know what it's like to have a different gender? A different skin color? Many projects nowadays allow you to take on the perspective of someone of a different gender or race by putting on a virtual reality headset.[8] You can (virtually) visit a doctor, take the subway, or interact with a salesperson as a woman rather than as a man, or as Black rather than as white.

These virtual experiences are a far cry from real experiences, of course, but they have been found to significantly reduce implicit racial bias.[9] One reason may be that biases and their effects suddenly become apparent, which induces dishabituation to discrimination.

These studies tell us that a visceral and intimate understanding of another person's experience produces dishabituation. Most people will not have access to such virtual reality tools, and it may be impossible to know how it really feels to be someone else, but we can gain a small window on another's existence through close friendships with members of another group. These can help to some extent, but for measurable change we need to find ways to make discrimination seem odd, unusual, and startling.

DISHABITUATION ENTREPRENEURS

If someone repeats a Jewish last name several times over dinner, and then refers to someone as the "Gentle Jew," the general reaction at the table could take multiple forms. It could be an appreciative laugh, a nod of recognition, or an expression of outrage. A laugh or a nod will not unsettle anything and might entrench it; an expression of outrage will disturb the impression of normalcy (and have a dishabituating effect).

A "natural" intervention that makes discrimination seem jarring and unfamiliar, a departure from what is normal and unremarkable, may be needed. Dishabituation entrepreneurs—people such as Margaret Sawyer, who are able to see the problem and react in real time—may be required to make the unseen seen. Sawyer is white, but she both observed the problematic nature of the Red Cross poster and pointed it out. Once she did that, others saw it as well and reacted. If a dishabituation entrepreneur had stood up at Cass's dinner party or Tali's science meeting, the incident would have been salient and altered people's expectations of what is acceptable.

In the history of civil rights in the United States, Rosa Parks was one such entrepreneur. On December 1, 1955, she famously refused to sit in the back of a bus in Montgomery, Alabama, signaling that racial segregation was a choice, not an inevitability, and that the choice oppressed Black people. That signal was heard loudly, not least by white people, some of whom became dishabituated to segregation.

Another dishabituation entrepreneur is Catharine MacKinnon. In 1978, she published *Sexual Harassment of Working Women*,[10] which has helped to define thinking about sex discrimination for decades. MacKinnon's book did three things at once. First, it essentially invented a new term: *sexual harassment*. The term was itself dishabituating. It named a practice that had previously gone uncharacterized.

Second, MacKinnon argued that sexual harassment was sex discrimination, and thus a violation of civil rights laws: a man who sexually harassed a woman was doing so *because she was a woman,* and was thus engaging in discrimination on the basis of sex.

That claim was also a form of dishabituation. Radical and new in 1978, MacKinnon's central argument was accepted by a unanimous Supreme Court as early as 1986, in an opinion written by Chief Justice William Rehnquist, a famous conservative: "When a supervisor sexually harasses a subordinate because of the subordinate's sex, that supervisor 'discriminates' on the basis of sex."[11]

Third, MacKinnon's book offered a set of narratives from women who had been subject to sexual harassment. The horrific details in the narratives put readers in the shoes of those who had been sexually harassed. After reading her book, people were not likely to be able to think that sexual harassment was an acceptable part of life.

The *canon of dishabituation,* as we might call it, could easily occupy a large library, including Betty Friedan's *The Feminine Mystique*[12] and Solomon Northup's *Twelve Years a Slave.*[13] What leads someone to become a dishabituation entrepreneur? Why Sawyer, Parks, Griffin, and MacKinnon—and not all the other people who sat on a segregated bus or observed or experienced sexual harassment? We are not aware of any research directly addressing this question. But certainly a combination of nature and nurture generates individuals who are less conformist, more skeptical, more courageous, and more perceptive. We like to think that becoming aware (via knowledge of behavioral science) of why and when people are unlikely to notice discrimination will increase the likelihood that more individuals will perceive the problems around them. Some people will also be courageous enough to try to fix those problems.

That leads to the next question: How can those dishabituation entrepreneurs help others dishabituate?

SURPRISED BY BIAS

As we stressed earlier, the brain is a predictive machine.[14] Its central mission is to predict, as accurately as possible, what will happen next so that it can prepare and react in time—to hide before the enemy arrives, hoard water before the drought, have an umbrella handy when it pours. We generate accurate predictions by watching and learning. We observe year after year that in November it rains more than in June, so we carry an umbrella during late fall rather than early summer.

We are constantly absorbing data from the world and consciously or unconsciously updating our judgments to enable us to make accurate predictions. At their best, our neurons are sophisticated biological calculators, keeping track of frequencies, means, associations, and more. So if, for example, most pilots we meet are men, we expect to see a male pilot when we get on a plane. When those expectations are met, there is no surprise signal in our brain alerting us that something is wrong.

From these statistical observations we then make assumptions about the underlying cause. If most pilots are males, our brain will quickly conclude that men are especially suited to flying a plane. If the "data" is biased because of historical discrimination, rather than reflecting some kind of truth about the capabilities of men and women, our conclusions will be biased because our brain is doing what it was built to do: deduce general rules based on perception.

Every day, we rely on such stereotypes and generalizations when making decisions. In deciding whom to hire, employers often use proxies of many sorts, even if those proxies are overbroad generalizations and far from entirely accurate. For example, test scores, employment records, level of education, and prestige of college attended are all part of what you may think of as rational factors in employment decisions. You might choose someone who went to a great university over someone who went to a good university, even though plenty of people who went to good universities would do better than plenty of people who went to great universities.

Race and sex often operate as similar proxies. Women may be more likely than men to be the primary caretakers of children and more likely to leave the employment market to take that role. If so, an employer might discriminate not because he dislikes or devalues women or is prejudiced in the ordinary sense, but because he believes (on the basis either of plausible assumptions or actual experience) that some stereotype is true enough to be a basis for employment decisions. Over time, such statistical discrimination can be a self-fulfilling prophecy. It can aggravate the very problem to which it is a response.

Matters can get even worse once you add artificial intelligence systems to the mix. AI systems are built to imitate the human mind—they use inputs from the world around them to make predictions and judgments.[15] If the data they receive is biased, AI systems will react like human beings: the decisions and recommendations they make will be biased.

Consider the experience of David and Jamie Heinemeier Hansson.[16] In 2019 the married couple applied for an Apple credit card. The two share all their financial resources, including bank accounts and property. They were thus astonished to learn that Apple offered David a much higher credit limit than it did to his wife, Jamie—twenty times higher. After sharing their story on social media, they discovered that others had experienced the same, including Apple cofounder Steve Wozniak and his wife.

Apple was using a biased machine-learning algorithm to assign credit. To develop credit-card scoring, an algorithm is fed millions of examples of good choices (for example, data on people who have paid their debt) and bad choices (for example, data on people who have not). It then learns which factors predict good choices. If females are paid less than males or find it more difficult to get a job because of gender discrimination, the algorithm will conclude that males are better candidates for credit. By discriminating against women, the algorithm will increase the gender gap further, creating a feedback loop.[17]

Once we detect a bias in AI systems, we can correct it by altering the algorithm directly or intentionally modifying the data used to create it. Although unable to tweak the algorithm our neurons use, we can debias the inputs they receive.

More than one hundred nations now have gender quotas designed to ensure that women are sufficiently represented in national legislatures. Some nations have quotas for members of national minorities, and some have imposed quotas designed to ensure that traditionally disadvantaged groups are represented in certain roles. Other public and private institutions are making efforts to increase racial or gender diversity in high-level positions and to ensure that portraits of prominent leaders include people of color and women. (It is true that in some nations, including the United States, serious legal questions are raised by efforts to consider race or gender in order to increase diversity.)

One dishabituation entrepreneur, Princeton neuroscience professor Yael Niv, has come up with a creative way to alert people to possible gender bias and nudge them toward more equal representation. She launched a website called BiasWatchNeuro (https://biaswatchneuro.com) that lists neuroscience conferences around the world, detailing the ratio of female-to-male speakers in each conference, and the names of the organizers. She then compares the speaker gender ratio to the expected ratio based on approximately how many females and males are in the field.

For example, the 31st International Behavioral Neuroscience Society Annual Meeting had 0 percent female speakers, even though 32 percent of the scientists in the field are female. Niv's list does not only make bias transparent; it also deprograms it. Organizers do not want their names associated with numbers suggestive of discrimination for all to see, so they make an effort to have adequate gender representation.

In a future world, where women scientists, pilots, politicians, and CEOs are as common as men, we would expect to see roughly the same number of females and males speaking at a conference, sitting in the cockpit, voting in Congress, and making decisions at the C-suite level. We will not notice gender in these contexts except when it *deviates* from roughly an equal ratio.

Think of it like this: if you observed the boxes below sequentially, by the time you get to the last box you would fully expect to observe five black arrows facing up and one white arrow facing down. If we recorded your brain activity when that last box is revealed, we would not see much. When there is nothing new, there is less signal.

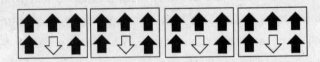

However, if we showed you the second sequence below, your neurons would fire wildly in response to the last box. You expected equal numbers of black arrows facing up and white arrows facing down, but got something completely different. You will likely pause to contemplate why reality did not match your expectations.

Niv is trying to reprogram our world so that in the future when we see one white arrow and five black arrows, we will be surprised and take note, because we will be used to the arrows being roughly half black ones facing up and half white ones facing down. She is doing this to reduce gender bias in the sciences, but her technique could be applied in any field, from business to government and the arts.

The roots of discrimination and bias are without doubt complex. They are spurred by history, economics, politics, and religion. But many of the roots can be traced back to the basic rules of how our brains work—those rules that govern what we see and what we miss, what we expect and what surprises us. Once we become aware of the rules, we can make seen what should be salient but is not, and perhaps make less salient what should be of no importance.

12

TYRANNY:

THE DEVASTATINGLY INCREMENTAL NATURE OF DESCENT INTO FASCISM

Each step was so small . . . one no more saw it developing from day to day than a farmer in his field sees the corn growing. One day it is over his head.

—ANONYMOUS GERMAN CITIZEN[1]

SUPPOSE THAT A NATION is moving toward tyranny.* Civil rights and civil liberties are at risk. Dissenters are targeted. Freedom of speech is under assault. Journalists and others are being intimidated, jailed, hurt, or even killed because they are thought to threaten the regime. All this happens gradually, not suddenly. Would people become habituated? How quickly?

---

* Sections of this chapter are adapted from C. R. Sunstein, *This Is Not Normal: The Politics of Everyday Expectations* (Yale University Press, 2021), and C. R. Sunstein, "It Can Happen Here," *New York Review of Books*, June 28, 2018.

To answer these questions, we might try to learn something from earlier turns to tyranny, perhaps above all from the rise of the Nazis in Germany in the 1930s. The problem is that Adolf Hitler's regime was so horrifying, and so unthinkably barbaric, that it is not easily recognizable to many contemporary readers. Many accounts of the period depict a barely imaginable series of events, a nation gone mad. That produces distance and even a kind of comfort. It is as if we are reading a dystopian science fiction novel in which Hitler is a character, not an actual figure from not-so-distant history.

But some depictions of Hitler's rise are intimate and personal. They focus less on historic figures, struggles for power, large events, state propaganda, murders, and war, and more on the details of individual lives. The depictions explore habituation in real time. They help explain not only how people can participate in terrible things but also how they can stand by quietly and live fairly ordinary days in the midst of them. For that reason, they offer lessons for people who now live in the midst of genuine horrors, but also and equally for those to whom horrors may never come but where democratic practices and norms are under severe pressure. The depictions tell us something important about the relationships among politics, habituation, and ordinary life, even when the political order is losing its moorings.

THE GRADUAL HABITUATION OF THE PEOPLE

Two such accounts of ordinary life under Nazism are offered by Milton Mayer's 1955 classic, *They Thought They Were Free*, and Sebastian Haffner's devastating, breathless, unfinished 1939 memoir, *Defying Hitler*, which gives a moment-by-moment, you-are-there feeling to Hitler's rise.[2] Rather than focusing on historic figures making transformative decisions, these accounts explore how people navigated their lives.

Haffner's real name was Raimund Pretzel. He used a pseudonym so as not to endanger his family in Germany while he was in exile in England. He was a journalist, not a historian or theorist, but he interrupts his riveting narrative to tackle a broad question: "What is history, and where does it take place?" Most works of history, he writes, give "the impression that no more than a few dozen people are involved, who happen to be 'at the helm of the ship of state' and whose deeds and decisions form what is called history."[3] In Haffner's view, that is wrong. "We anonymous others" are not just "pawns in the chess game."

On the contrary, the "most powerful dictators, ministers and generals are powerless against the simultaneous mass decisions taken individually and almost unconsciously by the population at large."[4] He insists on the importance of investigating "some very peculiar, very revealing, mental processes and experiences" involving "the private lives, emotions, and thoughts of individual Germans." Those private lives, emotions, and thoughts, in his account, are both peculiar and revealing in part because they show how people deal with cataclysmic political upheaval, and also with horror. Haffner was not a psychologist or a neuroscientist, but his focus was directly on mental processes, emotions, and thoughts, and he had a lot to say about habituation.

An American journalist of German descent, Mayer tried to

meet with Adolf Hitler in 1935. Mayer failed, but he did travel widely in Nazi Germany. He was stunned to discover something like a mass movement rather than the tyranny of a diabolical few. For that reason, he concluded that his original plan was all wrong. His real interest was not in Hitler but in humanity—in people like himself, to whom "something had happened that had not (or at least not yet) happened to me and my fellow country-men."[5] In 1952 he returned to Germany to find out what made Nazism possible, and to explore when and whether democracy could collapse into fascism, and how people reacted and habituated to it in real time.

To get clarity on that, Mayer decided to hone in. He focused on ten people, different in many respects but with one characteristic in common: they had all been members of the Nazi Party. Eventually they agreed to talk, accepting his explanation that as an American of German ancestry, he hoped to give the people of his nation a better understanding of Germany. Mayer was truthful about that and about nearly everything else. But he was not forthcoming about a central point: he did not tell them he was a Jew.

In the late 1930s—the period that most interested Mayer—his subjects were working as a janitor; a soldier; a cabinetmaker; an office manager; a baker; a bill collector; an inspector; a high school teacher; and a police officer. One had been a high school student. All of them were male. None had occupied a position of leadership or influence. All of them referred to themselves as *wir kleine Leute* (we little people). They lived in Marburg, a university town situated on the river Lahn, not far from Frankfurt.

Mayer talked with them over the course of a year, under

informal conditions—coffee, meals, and long, relaxed evenings. He became friends with each (and throughout, he refers to them as such). As he put it, with evident surprise, "I *liked* them. I couldn't help it." They could be ironic, funny, and self-deprecating. Most of them enjoyed a joke that originated in Nazi Germany: "What is an Aryan?" "An Aryan is a man who is tall like Hitler, blond like Goebbels, and lithe like Göring."

They could also be street-smart. Speaking of the views of ordinary people under Hitler, one of them asked, "Opposition? . . . How would anybody know? How would anybody know what somebody else opposes or doesn't oppose? That a man *says* he opposes or doesn't oppose depends upon the circumstances, where, and when, and to whom, and just how he says it. And then you must still guess *why* he says what he says."[6]

Mayer's new friend was referring to the idea, mentioned in chapter 10, of "preference falsification": people often fail to say what they like and think, at least in public, because of existing social norms (or official threats).[7] Preference falsification can be found everywhere, including in democracies. It is one reason that political systems, and any status quo, can be far more fragile than people think. When authoritarianism is gaining a foothold, preference falsification runs rampant, which contributes to habituation. This is because if people do not know that other people are concerned or enraged, they will be more likely to get used to what they are observing and take it as normal. As months and years went past, people habituated to aspects of Nazism that they did not much like.

Mayer's most stunning conclusion is that with one partial

exception (the teacher), none of his subjects "saw Nazism as we—you and I—saw it *in any respect*." Where most of us understand Nazism as a form of tyranny, enslaving or murdering its citizens and violating human rights, Mayer's subjects "did not know before 1933 that Nazism was evil. They did not know between 1933 and 1945 that it was evil. And they do not know it now." Seven years after the war, they looked back on Hitler's prewar years as the best time of their lives.

In Mayer's account, human beings focus on their own lives and "the sights that meet them in their daily rounds." Democratic norms can be undermined, and democracy can collapse, for just that reason.

Mayer did not bring up anti-Semitism with any of his subjects, but after a few meetings, each of them did so on his own, and they returned to it constantly. When the local synagogue was burned in 1938, most of the community felt only one obligation: *"not to interfere."* Eventually Mayer showed his friends an issue of the local newspaper, from November 11, 1938, which contained a report: "In the interest of their own security, a number of male Jews were taken into custody yesterday. This morning they were sent away from the city." None of Mayer's friends remembered seeing it, or indeed anything like it.

With evident fatigue, the baker reported, "One had no time to think. There was so much going on." His account tracked that of Mayer's colleague, a German philologist in the country at the time, who emphasized the devastatingly incremental nature of the descent into tyranny and said, "We had no time to think about these dreadful things that were growing, little by little, all around us."

The philologist pointed to a regime bent on diverting its people, through endless self-celebrations and dramas (often involving real or imagined enemies), and "the gradual habituation of the people, little by little." In his account, "Each step was so small, so inconsequential, so well explained, or, on occasion, so regretted," that people could no more see it "developing from day-to-day than a farmer in his field sees the corn growing. One day it is over his head."[8]

THE AUTOMATIC CONTINUATION
OF ORDINARY LIFE

Focusing largely on 1933, Haffner offers a complementary picture. Just twenty-five years old in that year and studying law with the goal of becoming a judge or an administrator, Haffner describes how his high-spirited friends and fellow students were preoccupied with fun, career prospects, and love affairs. Some aggressive actions, aimed at political dissenters, started early, but citizens were simultaneously distracted by an endless stream of festivities and celebrations. People flirted, enjoyed romance, "went to the cinema, had a meal in a small wine bar, drank Chianti, and went dancing together." This "automatic continuation of ordinary life" promoted habituation and hindered any organized, forceful reaction against the horror.[9]

In Haffner's telling, the collapse of freedom and the rule of law occurred in increments, some of which seemed relatively insignificant. Germany did not turn on a dime. Haffner believed that, even though the full measure of Nazism unfolded over time, its true nature was evident and known to some Germans from the very start—though they did not know what it would eventually do.

The point holds as well for the reactions of Jews themselves. In 1933, when Nazi officers stood menacingly outside Jewish shops, Jews were merely "offended." Not worried or anxious. Just "offended." It is reasonable to think that feeling mere offense—unaccompanied by worry or anxiety, let alone terror—was a reasonable initial reaction. Still, Haffner argues that Hitler's brutality, and the coming politicization of everyday life, was clear to some from the outset. In the early days of his regime, a self-styled republican advised Haffner to avoid skeptical comments because they were of no use: "I think I know the fascists better than you. We republicans must howl with the wolves."[10]

Books started to disappear from bookshops and libraries. Journals and newspapers slowly disappeared as well, and those that remained kept to the party line. As early as 1933, Germans who refused to become Nazis found themselves "in a fiendish situation: it was one of complete and unalleviated hop[e]lessness; you were daily subjected to insults and humiliation."[11]

EACH ACT IS WORSE THAN THE LAST, BUT ONLY A LITTLE

Precisely because of the fine-grained, even intimate nature of their accounts, Mayer and Haffner speak directly to those concerned about what makes liberty and democracy vulnerable. We can't know whether to believe Mayer's subjects when they claimed ignorance of what Hitler actually did. Mayer isn't sure either. But the subjects are convincing when they say that what happened was a form of slow habituation.

One of the German citizens to whom Mayer spoke said, "Each act, each occasion, is worse than the last, but only a little worse. . . . If the last and worst act of the whole regime had come immediately after the first and smallest, thousands, yes, millions would have been sufficiently shocked. . . . But of course this isn't the way it happens. In between come all the hundreds of little steps, some of them imperceptible, each of them preparing you to not be shocked by the next. Step C is not so much worse than Step B, and, if you did not make a stand at Step B, why should you at Step C? And so on to Step D."[12]

Step D was the murdering of millions by the Nazi regime. But the genocide did not start with Step D. It began with Step A—restrictions on the legal, economic, and social rights of German Jews, which gradually and steadily accumulated throughout the 1930s. On April 1, 1933, Jewish-owned businesses were boycotted. Soon thereafter, Jewish lawyers were disbarred and Jews were prohibited from being journalists. A few months later, a law was passed authorizing physicians to conduct involuntary sterilizations on Jews. Numerous other restrictions were put in place, and violent acts occurred until 1939, when Hitler authorized involuntary euthanasia of mentally and physically disabled people, which eventually led to systematic mass executions.

We have seen that habituation happens when an event

is constant, frequent, or changing only very gradually. Even a large explosion might be overlooked if it is preceded by a slightly smaller one, which is preceded by an even smaller one. But if people encounter an "explosion" without being exposed to the preceding steps, they will not have the opportunity to habituate and may therefore be more likely to react.

This is often the experience of outsiders, who become aware of a horrific situation beyond their immediate environment only at Step D, without being directly exposed to Steps A, B, and C. Those who look on with horror from the outside (such as citizens observing horrors abroad) may thus be less vulnerable to habituation, as they were not exposed to all the steps along the way and may choose to be upstanders—helping those who need help, and working to combat those who cause harm—rather than bystanders.

Haffner argues that some people on the inside can see what is happening early, perhaps from a combination of disposition and experience, perhaps from prescience or recalcitrance. Some Jews were in this category and left Germany before it was too late. Haffner puts himself in this camp as well: "As for the Nazis, my nose left me with no doubts. It was just tiresome to talk about which of their alleged goals and intentions were still acceptable or even 'historically justified' when all of it stank. How it stank! That the Nazis were enemies, my enemies and the enemies of all I held dear, was crystal clear to me from the outset."[13]

But often this camp is not large enough. Habituation, confusion, distraction, self-interest, fear, rationalization, and a sense of personal powerlessness make terrible things possible. They help explain not only the rise of Nazism, but also the disintegration of democracy, and the loss of freedom, in many places.

HABITUATING THE JOHNSONS?

How common is habituation to horror? You might think that we cannot draw general lessons from what happened in Germany in the 1930s. If you take the average Jane and the standard Joe and increase appalling acts ever so gradually, what percentage would go along with those acts? What fraction would participate, and how many would fight back?

To answer these questions, consider the following scenario (the account may sound familiar to you, but we are about to offer a new twist on an old tale):[14]

On a warm August day, you enter the old brown-brick building of the psychology department at Yale University to take part in an experiment.[15] The researcher, who recruited you early that week, informed you that the study's aim was to examine the effects of punishment on memory.

Upon arrival you are greeted by said researcher, who leads you into a room with one other volunteer. The researcher explains that you will complete the experiment in tandem with that volunteer, who will sit in an adjacent room. You will take on the role of a teacher and your partner will be a student. The student will be given a list of word pairs to memorize. When the student makes a mistake, you are to a press a button on a fancy-looking machine that will deliver a shock to the student, strapped to an electric chair.

The shock generator clearly delineates thirty voltage levels, ranging from 15 to 450 volts. Next to each level is a description, ranging from SLIGHT SHOCK (near the lowest voltage) to DANGER: SEVERE SHOCK (near the highest voltage). "Although the shocks can be extremely painful, they cause no permanent tissue damage," the researcher assures you both, and asks you to try it on your arm at the lowest voltage. After testing it, you agree that it's not that bad. So, the experiment begins!

You provide your student with the first test word over the intercom: "Breadsticks." The student answers correctly, "Fish fingers." You provide the second word: "Windfall." "Dinosaur," tries the student. That's wrong, so the researcher instructs you to press a button to deliver an electric shock of the lowest voltage. With each additional mistake the student makes, you must ramp up the voltage by fifteen volts: 30, 45, 60, 75. At 75 you hear small grunts from the other room, but you continue: 90, 105, 120. At that point the student shouts.

At 150 the student cries out, "Experimenter, get me out of here! I won't be in the experiment anymore! I refuse to go on!" At 180 the student blurts, "I can't stand the pain." At 270 the student screams and at 300 refuses to answer questions. After 330 the student cannot be heard anymore. At which point do you stop delivering shocks?

As you may have noticed, the scenario above mimics the famous series of experiments conducted in 1961 by Yale psychologist Stanley Milgram.[16] Milgram's "student" was a confederate working for Milgram. In his initial experiment Milgram reported that 65 percent of participants went up to a 450-volt shock, which was two steps beyond DANGER: SEVERE SHOCK. In a later experiment 62 percent of the participants went to the maximum level. Milgram's participants were unlikely to be outliers. They came from a range of occupations, including engineers, high school teachers, and postal clerks. Though they only included men, the basic findings were generally replicated in 2009 (with only slightly lower obedience rates) in both men and women.[17]

Milgram's goal was to understand the rise of authoritarianism, as clearly displayed in Germany during World War II. He wanted to study obedience and to understand how people could participate in horrible acts. Indeed, his experiments tell us something important about obedience. But intentionally or unintentionally, Milgram was also studying habituation.

Imagine if Milgram had asked his volunteers to deliver the maximum voltage at the very beginning. How many people would comply? We suspect the numbers would have been much lower. By asking the "teachers" to up the voltage one step at a time, from A to B to C to D, Milgram was inducing habituation. The teachers may have felt some guilt at Step A (when providing a fifteen-volt shock), but that guilt subsided with every additional shock administered. By the time the teachers reached Step D (the high voltage) they had adapted to the idea and guilt of causing another person dreadful pain.

Providing shocks in a controlled laboratory at Yale is a far cry from participating in (or observing) genocide, but we suspect that a similar principle plays a role in both. When horrors start small and increase gradually, they elicit a weaker emotional reaction, less resistance, and more acceptance, allowing larger and larger horrors to play out in broad daylight. Awareness of this phenomenon may enable more people to foresee what is coming and to take action in time.

13

LAW:

PUTTING A PRICE ON PAIN?

A FEW YEARS AGO, CASS was walking home in Concord, Massachusetts, on a cold, dark, and snowy night. Cass crossed the street to get some pizza for his son, then crossed it again to take the quickest route home.

The next thing he knew, Cass woke up in what appeared to be a hospital. His body was attached to various machines. His head hurt; his arms hurt; his legs hurt. Everything hurt. His chest hurt most of all. He could barely move. He thought, "There are two possibilities here. The first is that I am in a hospital, and it's really not good. The second is that I am just having one of those dreams. It seems much more likely that I am dreaming." Comfortable with that conclusion, Cass went right back to sleep. A few hours later, he woke up again. He was still in a hospital. The same one. Everything still hurt. It wasn't a dream.

The doctor informed Cass that he had been hit by a car, going about forty miles per hour. "You should be relieved; you could easily have been killed," the doctor said. Cass didn't feel so relieved. In a quiet, matter-of-fact voice, the doctor continued, "You have a severe concussion and plenty of broken bones." The doctor then asked Cass if he could wriggle his toes. Cass obliged, and the doctor smiled brightly with evident relief.

The doctor explained that Cass had been asleep for a full twelve hours, and while his injuries were numerous and bad, all of the initial signs pointed to a complete recovery. It would be a difficult few weeks, and possibly a difficult few months. But before long, Cass would be fine.

The doctor's prediction was right. The recovery was rapid, though the first weeks were not a lot of fun, with a fair bit of pain and more than a little suffering. During those weeks, the local police gave Cass numerous details about how, exactly, the accident had happened.

Visibility on the street that Cass crossed was quite poor, amid the snowstorm, and apparently the driver who hit Cass hadn't seen him or slowed down. Some of Cass's friends wondered if he would sue the driver for compensation.

Cass had absolutely no interest in doing that. But if the driver had indeed been careless—if, for example, he had been going over the speed limit and not watching the road—Cass might have been able to obtain a lot of money for "pain and suffering," meaning the misery that he experienced as a result of the injury. He might also have been able to get "hedonic damages," for the lost enjoyment of life during his recovery. (No running, no jumping, less walking, no tennis, less fun.)

In many legal systems, you can receive money for pain and

suffering and for the diminished enjoyment of life stemming from assaults, road accidents, food poisoning from a restaurant, sexual harassment at work, and so forth. Some people end up with a lot of money that way. Roughly speaking, "pain and suffering" are about experienced *un*happiness (a difficult hour or day), whereas "hedonic damages" are about lost happiness (an inability to enjoy certain activities).

So if you are hit by a car and spend a few weeks getting better, you will undoubtedly experience a lot of pain and suffering. The legal system will ask, How much money would you have to be paid so that you aren't worse off than if you had never been hit? You might be tempted to say, "Are you kidding? No amount is high enough!"

That might be right. But surely it's better to be compensated than not to be compensated, and if you didn't suffer all that much, maybe some sum of money does compensate you for those not-good weeks. Even if you suffered a lot, maybe a massive sum of money will provide a high degree of compensation. At least that is the hope.

With respect to hedonic damages, the point is that if you have been hurt, you have probably lost something, including activities you like or love. Maybe you can't run for a few months. Money is supposed to compensate you for the loss—to get you to the place, in terms of overall well-being, where you would have been if you had not been injured. Maybe no amount of money can get you there, at least for the most terrible losses. But the goal is to try to restore people to the level of well-being that they would have enjoyed had the injury not occurred.

Compensation is also supposed to create deterrence. It

will encourage people to drive more safely, to reduce the risk of food poisoning, to produce medicines without harmful side effects.

To identify the right award, juries and judges must answer some hard questions about the nature and quality of people's experiences. They need to figure out what eight weeks of recovery from an automobile accident are like, and then turn that knowledge into a monetary figure. Is the right number $10,000? $50,000? $100,000? $200,000? More? How could a jury or a judge know? Even with his personal experience, Cass himself had no idea.

By now, you probably know that because people habituate, they are likely to suffer a lot less, and lose a lot less happiness, than they would if they did not habituate. But this is not intuitive. Studies clearly show that we underestimate habituation when we predict how terrible events will affect us and others. Imagine, for example, that someone has lost two fingers, and the legal system is asked to monetize the losses, including for pain and suffering. When you think about it, the idea of losing two fingers seems pretty horrible. But because of habituation, the effects of such a loss on people's actual experience, from day to day or month to month, might not be nearly as severe as they imagine.

After a period of adjustment and transition, those who lose two fingers may not be much worse off in how they feel than those who suffer no such loss. Actually they might not be worse off at all (remarkably, some studies suggest that no difference can be discerned in measures of well-being between ordinary people and those who have lost a limb).[1] Juries and judges, like everyone else, will underestimate people's ability to habituate to a hand with three fingers. For that reason, they will probably exaggerate the magnitude of emotional losses.

These types of mistakes are aggravated by what is known as the *focusing illusion*. The basic idea is that when you think of one aspect of your life, you often exaggerate its importance. You think that it has a larger impact than it actually does. As Daniel Kahneman puts it, "Nothing in life is as important as you think it is when you are thinking about it."[2]

For example, both people who live there and people who do not tend to believe that people are happier in California.[3] But those who live in California have been found not to be happier than those who live elsewhere. Focusing on California weather in particular, people who live in California and people who live in Ohio believe that they would be happier in California—even though data shows that weather is not an especially important determinant of most people's happiness. The general point is that people focus on a particular loss or gain without seeing that after the loss or gain has occurred, they are not likely to focus much on it. When "primed" to think about weather, or any other factor that is a relatively small ingredient in most people's happiness (such as, for example, the ability to perform well in sports), focusing illusions lead people to give excessive weight to that factor.

When asked to award damages for a loss, the attention of the jury and the judge is fixed on the loss in question. It is as if juries were asked, "Would you be happier in California?" Focused keenly on a particular injury, juries and judges are unlikely to see that, most of the time, people may not be much focused on that injury in their daily lives. The very circumstances of a trial invite people to neglect habituation and create the focusing illusion.* It is not difficult to find cases of sizable pain and suffering awards that may have been influenced in this way:[4] for example, a $1 million award for the loss of feeling and strength in a hand,[5] or a $1.5 million award for disfigured hands.[6]

The same logic follows for hedonic damages. Suppose that someone has lost mobility so that she can no longer ski or play soccer. Skiing is great, and so is soccer. But if the question is how much that person has lost in "enjoyment of life," the answer might well be "not nearly as much as you think."

To be clear, as Cass himself can attest, the short-term harm might be severe even if habituation means that the long-term harm is smaller than expected. In the short run, people might experience a level of distress, fear, mourning, and grief for which significant compensation is justified. Big monetary awards might well be given for short periods of intense suffering or sense of loss.

Moreover, habituation does not always occur, and even if

---

* This is true for plaintiffs as well as for juries. Those who bring suit will likely focus on their injury—likely more so than those who do not bring suit. It might even make sense to discourage (some) plaintiffs from bringing suit because litigation will prevent habituation.

it does, it might be only partial. In some cases judges or juries may be awarding insufficient sums. It may be especially
difficult, for example, to habituate to physical pain, and some
individuals never do. Suppose that a plaintiff is suffering
chronic back pain. The pain may be relatively low grade, but
if it is persistent, it can be terrible. It is not difficult to find
cases in which juries have awarded low damages in analogous
instances. For example:

- $4,000 for an accident producing headaches three to
  four times per week and persistent pain in the hands,
  knees, and shoulders.[7]
- $25,000 to a nineteen-year-old woman whose accident
  caused hip disfigurement and back pain.[8]
- $30,000 for permanent pain in the neck from a herniated
  cervical spinal disc and in the knee from a torn menis-
  cus.[9]

In each case, the award seems far too low because habituation may not occur or may be limited, ensuring that the injury
is likely to be enduring. When you first think about it, low-level
back pain, headaches, ringing in the ears, and pain in the neck
or knee may not seem especially serious. These are familiar
to many of us, unlike the loss of a limb. It is easy to imagine
a judge or jury concluding that while headaches are unpleasant, they can be part of daily life, whereas the loss of a limb is
devastating. But if people fail to habituate to headaches, ringing in the ears, and similar conditions, they will suffer massive

losses, which judges or jurors may not appreciate. Moreover, if the incident produces depression or anxiety, these mental health problems will slow the process of habituation (as we saw in chapter 4). The emotional injury may be large, and significant damage awards are justified. Yet judges and jurors might well fail to see this point.

CAPABILITIES

The very ideas of "pain and suffering" and "hedonic damages" suggest that what matters is whether people are miserable or losing out on pleasure. (In many nations, the law speaks in exactly those terms.) But as we have seen, *emotional states are not all that matter*. The legal system should be, and is, attentive to that. Suppose you lose the use of a leg, and after a difficult but short period of adaptation, you are as happy as you were before the loss. Should the law disregard your injury?

Absolutely not. You cannot walk on your leg; you certainly are unable to run. You are unable to engage in many activities that you used to take for granted. You may not be in pain, and you may not be suffering or sad. Nonetheless, you have lost a capability.[10] You should be awarded damages for that loss. The loss is real and significant, even if measures of your emotional states are unable to identify it. Consider the fact that there is a great deal of evidence that people strongly prefer to be in a healthy state, even after they have habituated to a health condition, and so are not suffering much or at all in hedonic terms.[11]

Those who lose physical or cognitive abilities suffer objective harm. People who have had colostomies or must receive kidney dialysis treatments several times a week have experienced a real loss, whatever their emotional state. Indeed, people with colostomies do not seem to have lower levels of happiness than people without colostomies, but they say that they would be willing to shorten their life span by up to 15 percent if they could live without a colostomy.[12] Similarly, dialysis patients do not seem to enjoy their days less than the rest of us, but many of them say that they would willingly subtract a significant number of their remaining years to have normal kidney function.[13]

It is also possible that patients too are vulnerable to focusing illusions, no less so than those in Chicago or Cleveland who think that they would be much better off if they were able to experience the weather enjoyed by people in Los Angeles. Still, the fact that patients would give up significant amounts of their lives to be well seems to suggest that they are experiencing real losses—capability losses—even if their emotional states are pretty good.

In a variety of cases, pain and suffering or hedonic damages are probably best understood as capability damages. For example, courts have awarded people a lot of money for losing the ability to engage in sports,[14] for the loss of the senses of taste and smell,[15] poor coordination,[16] and for the loss of sexual function.[17] In cases of this kind, courts may have believed that the plaintiffs were far less happy. If so, they may not have been right. But all of the plaintiffs lost a set of capabilities and deserved significant damages for that reason.

If people are unable to walk or run or to participate in athletic activities, their lives have been impaired, even if they have habituated to the impairments. If people habituate to losses, their lives will go much better than they otherwise would. But even so, losses remain losses. People deserve to be compensated for them.

14

EXPERIMENTS IN LIVING:

THE FUTURE OF DISHABITUATION

It is useful that while mankind are imperfect
there should be different opinions, so is it that
there should be different experiments of living.

—JOHN STUART MILL[1]

N 1271 A YOUNG Italian man by the name of Marco left his
hometown of Venice on a journey to China. The excursion
was rough; Marco had to climb mountains and cross a large
desert. At times food was scarce and water limited. He became ill along the way. But he was set on reaching his destination, and after approximately four grueling years he did.[2] He
was one of few Italians to do so.

Seven hundred forty-six years later, another Italian by
the name of Marco left his home country for China. He too
crossed deserts and mountains, but he did so in a jet plane
rather than on foot. He ate a nice chicken dinner and drank
a glass of white wine, binge-watched a show, and took a nap.
When he awoke, he was in Beijing. It took him nine hours and

thirteen minutes to reach his destination. He was one of approximately a quarter million Italians to do so that year.

Five years later, a third young man by the name of Marco
was lounging in his apartment in Venice. He put on a headset
and within seconds found himself at the Great Wall of China.
He spent the next thirty-two minutes exploring the magnifi-
cent architectural feat and chatting with locals along the way.
He was one of millions of Italians to experience virtual reality.

Today your brain can travel to different places on earth (and
beyond) with great ease in minutes. Using the internet or virtual
reality, you can submerge your mind in cultures and places different from your own and connect with people of varying beliefs
and norms. You can also physically visit these places in hours via
the miracle of commercial flights to experience smells, sounds,
and sights you have never smelled, heard, or seen before.

Yet, not that long ago most people would spend the en-
tirety of their lifetimes within a few square miles of where they
were born. The Marcos, Marys, Toms, Abrahams, Saras, and
Francescas living hundreds and thousands of years ago were
exposed to one dialect, one culture, one type of cuisine, and
one kind of scenery. They viewed their existences as natural,
inevitable, and fixed. They became habituated to whatever
surrounded them. Most could not imagine that other possible
realities existed. Some of their beliefs were wrong, and some
of their customs were cruel. But without comparisons to other
notions and norms, it was difficult to notice what could be
improved and how. Being defined and limited by their experience, they could not easily see what deserved to be applauded
and celebrated, and what required scrutiny and reassessment.

To be sure, your ancestors included individuals with vary-ing beliefs, preferences, and ideas. Yet it would have been im-mensely difficult for your ancestors to see that their God was one of many possible objects of worship, or that 60°F is cold if you live in Senegal but warm if you live in Sweden. To open your ancestors to competing perspectives, which would en-able them to rethink what they wrongly took for granted, "ex-periments in living" were required.

We adapt this term from John Stuart Mill's celebration of "experiments of living."[*3] Mill often emphasized the impor-tance of seeing one's beliefs, values, norms, and situations from a distance, so as to be able to evaluate them and perhaps learn that a change would be desirable.[4]

You cannot know for certain what is good or bad for you, your family, or your community through your intuitions, based on limited experience. This is partly because of the rules that govern the function and architecture of your brain. The algo-rithms of your mind can make it difficult to notice the marvels and demons around you when environments, norms, and be-haviors are fixed and unvaried. How, then, can you know what is best for your life and for society, what needs to be changed, and what should be celebrated?

Think about it like this: How do you know if smoking causes cancer? How do you know if a silver coin will float

---

* Thus Mill pointed to "the value, in the present low state of human improve-ment, of placing human beings in contact with persons dissimilar to them-selves, and with modes of thought and action unlike those with which they are familiar."

on a calm blue lake? How do you know whether lemon pie is tasty? You experiment. You taste the pie, place the coin on the water, and compare the longevity of smokers to that of nonsmokers. In important respects, the same approach holds for concepts of good and bad. These concepts need to be tested by the experiences you have in seeing them up close and maybe even living them out, not merely by comparing them with your intuitions.*

True, life is short and resources are limited, so you cannot experiment firsthand with all forms of living to find those beliefs and ways of life that are optimal for you. This is where the Marco Polos of the world come in.

Marco Polo lived a varied life—a psychologically rich life. He left Europe for Asia at a time when doing so was both difficult and rare. He experienced a completely different world. He dishabituated. Every aspect of the new world shaped how he viewed aspects of his old world. How he perceived governance, family, marriage, cruelty, wisdom, and beauty altered. His ability to detect certain tastes and sounds changed too.

The reason is obvious. How you value and perceive objects, concepts, and events, and even whether you notice them at all, depends on context. Values and perceptions depend on which other objects or events you experience at the same time and which you have experienced in the past. (Recall here our epi-

---

* We are not seeking to make any controversial philosophical claims here about the components of a good life. The simple point is that it is hard to know what is good and what is bad without having a sense of the alternatives.

graph from H. G. Wells: "A thousand things that had seemed unnatural and repulsive speedily became natural and ordinary to me. I suppose everything in existence takes its colour from the average hue of our surroundings."[5]

For example, whether you will judge faces as threatening depends on what other faces you are seeing.[6] When very threatening faces are all around you, you habituate to those faces; as a result, you will start perceiving mildly threatening faces as neutral. When very threatening faces are rare, you might perceive mildly threatening faces as very threatening indeed. Or imagine you are tasked with deciding which research proposals are ethical and which are not. If many clearly unethical proposals are in the pile, you are more likely to approve proposals that are questionable, but not clearly unethical. Valuation and perception depend on what is prevalent, so if different things become prevalent, your perception will change, and so will your views of what is right and wrong.[7]

Marco Polo drastically changed the context within which he was operating, and when he returned to Italy after twenty-four years away, he was no longer habituated to European customs. But here is the important part—these "experiments of living" of one man did not change only that one man. Polo shared his observations with others back home, first orally and later in a book, *The Travels of Marco Polo*,[8] detailing his journeys. In that sense he was a dishabituation entrepreneur.

The book, which was written by Rustichello da Pisa from stories told to him by Polo, described to Europeans a different culture, and a different world, from their own. The book was a huge success. It offered readers a new perspective through which to observe their own lives. It allowed them to dishabituate, to move their eyes and notice the colors around them that they could not see before. It enabled them to turn off the gray scale. "Experiments in living" allow both the experimenter (Polo) and the observer (the reader) to reassess their own lives in a fresh light, and to reevaluate beliefs that might have become frozen.

Nowadays it is much easier to be the experimenter as well as the observer. More than at any other point in history, human beings can be placed in contact with people different from themselves, and with modes of thought and action with which they are unfamiliar. One reason is the relative ease of international travel. If you live in a city or a nation that is facing terrible problems (high crime rates, dirty air, high levels of poverty, corruption), you can easily see, up close, cities and nations that do not face those problems. If you live in a city or a nation that is wondrous in multiple ways, you can easily see, up close, cities and nations that are not so wondrous.

While there may not be a substitute for physical presence, you do not have to travel to come into contact with different kinds of people and different ways of life. You can do something like that online, encountering texts, images, videos, and virtual realities that might jolt you. What you encounter might be revolting or it might be thrilling. But in either case, it might well enable you to see your own situation, and your own life, in a fresh light, to be surprised by what was there right in front of you.

Yogi Berra, the great baseball player, once said, "It's tough to make predictions, especially about the future." We agree.

Still, current and emerging technologies promise to bring diverse beliefs and traditions up close. We can readily imagine a future in which people can experience, in a day or even a morning, all sorts of different realities, separating them from their own experiences and putting those experiences in a new light.

Those technologies might serve as "dishabituation machines," transporting us away from our reality and back again. In some cases, the results will be unsettling and unpleasant. We will suddenly see terrible things as such. But in other cases, we hope, our world will resparkle.

ACKNOWLEDGMENTS

WE ARE GRATEFUL TO many people for their help with this book. Julia Cheiffetz, our editor at One Signal, saw promise in our idea from the beginning and masterfully guided us from conception to final draft. Julia's direction and notes were invaluable. Sameer Rahim, our editor at Little, Brown, also provided us with insightful comments and offered welcome optimism. We are grateful to the bright Tim Whiting, for his confidence in this book and prior work. We are grateful as well to Ida Rothschild for taking a good, hard look at the book at a late stage and for suggesting many changes that led to significant improvements.

This book would not have come to life without our extraordinary agents, Heather Schroder (Compass Talent), Sophie Lambert (Conville and Walsh), Sarah Chalfant (Wylie Agency), and Rebecca Nagel (Wylie Agency). We are fortunate to have these strong and intelligent women by our sides, not only as agents who fight for our work, but also as caring, smart friends.

We are grateful to Amir Doron for pointing us toward some of the most interesting stories in this book and to Mani Ramaswami and Lucile Kellis for helpful discussion. We thank Oren Bar-Gill, Laura Globig, Eric Posner, Liron Rozenkrantz,

Mark Tushnet, and Valentina Vellani for valuable comments on an early draft. We also owe a large thank-you to the brilliant students at the Affective Brain Lab whose research is described in this book: Neil Garrett, Hadeel Haj Ali, Chris Kelly, Bastien Blain, Laura Globig, Valentina Vellani, Stephanie Lazzaro, Sara Zheng, Nora Holtz, Irene Cogliati Dezza, Moshe Glickman, and India Pinhorn. We are also grateful to Harvard Law School and its Program on Behavioral Economics and Public Policy, and Dean John Manning, for support of various kinds. Finally, we thank Kathleen Rizzo and Victoria Yu for heroic work in bringing this book to completion.

From Tali: Huge thank-you to my family for support. I am lucky to have a brilliant mind by my side daily—my husband, Josh McDermott—in whose opinions I trust like no other. This book is dedicated to our wondrous, loving, and kind children, Livia and Leo. My love for them all will never habituate.

From Cass: Special thanks to my wife, Samantha Power, for wisdom, humor, and kindness, and for many discussions of this project. My young children, Declan and Rían, were patient and engaged interlocutors, and my older child, Ellyn, was a great friend throughout; they join Livia and Leo as dedicatees. My Labrador Retrievers, Snow and Finley, were with me throughout and made their way into this book at various stages (subtly, I hope).

NOTES

1. H. G. Wells and J. Roberts, *The Island of Dr. Moreau* (Project Gutenberg, 2009), 136.

Introduction: How We Habituate to Everything, All the Time

1. Vincent Gaston Dethier, *The Hungry Fly: A Physiological Study of the Behavior Associated with Feeding* (Cambridge, MA: Harvard University Press, 1976), 411. A note on style: We offer a large number of notes and references here, often with page references; where the specific point or quotation is straightforward to find, we follow convention and refer to the source more broadly.

2. M. Ramaswami, "Network Plasticity in Adaptive Filtering and Behavioral Habituation," *Neuron* 82 (6) (June 18, 2014): 1216–29.

3. "New Study Finds What Triggers the 'Holiday Feeling,'" *Travel Bulletin*, 2019, https://www.travelbulletin.co.uk/news-mainmenu/new-study-finds-what-triggers-the-holiday-feeling.

4. Wikipedia, s.v. "Dagen H."

5. A. Dembosky, "Can Virtual Reality Be Used to Combat Racial Bias in Health Care?," KQED, April 2021, https://www.kqed.org/news/11898973/can-virtual-reality-help-combat-racial-bias-in-health-care VR reduces bias.

6. H. Allcott et al., "The Welfare Effects of Social Media," *American Economic Review* 110 (3) (2020): 629–76.

7. B. Cavalazzi et al., "Cellular Remains in a ~3.42-Billion-Year-Old Subsea-floor Hydrothermal Environment," *Science Advances* 7 (9) (2021); and Matthew S. Dodd et al., "Evidence for Early Life in Earth's Oldest Hydro-thermal Vent Precipitates," *Nature* 543 (7643) (2017): 60–64.

8. B. T. Juang et al., "Endogenous Nuclear RNAi Mediates Behavioral Adaptation to Odor," *Cell* 154 (5) (2013): 1010–22; and D. L. Noelle et al., "The Cyclic GMP-Dependent Protein Kinase EGL-4 Regulates Olfactory Adaptation in *C. elegans*," *Neuron* 36 (6) (2002): 1079–89.

9. Carl Zimmer, "How Many Cells Are in Your Body?," *National Geographic*, October 23, 2013, https://www.nationalgeographic.com/science/article /how-many-cells-are-in-your-body#:~:text=37.2%20trillion%20cells ,,magnitude%20except%20in%20the%20movies.

10. Eric R. Kandel et al., eds., *Principles of Neural Science*, 5th ed. (New York: McGraw-Hill, 2013); and W. G. Regehr, "Short-Term Presynaptic Plasticity," *Cold Spring Harbor Perspectives in Biology* 4 (7) (2012): a005702.

11. I. P. V. Troxler, "On the Disappearance of Given Objects from Our Visual Field," ed. K. Himly and J. A. Schmidt, *Ophthalmologische Bibliothek* 2 (2) (1804): 1–53.

12. J. Benda, "Neural Adaptation," *Current Biology* 31 (3) (2021): R110–R116.

13. A. S. Bristol and T. J. Carew, "Differential Role of Inhibition in Habituation of Two Independent Afferent Pathways to a Common Motor Output," *Learning & Memory* 12 (1) (2005): 52–60.

14. E. N. Sokolov, "Higher Nervous Functions: The Orienting Reflex," *Annual Review of Physiology* 25 (1) (1963): 545–80.

15. A. Ishai et al., "Repetition Suppression of Faces Is Modulated by Emotion," *Proceedings of the National Academy of Sciences of the USA* 101 (2004): 9827–32.

1: Happiness: On Ice Cream, the Midlife Crisis, and Monogamy

1. David Marchese, "Julia Roberts Hasn't Changed. But Hollywood Has," *New York Times*, April 18, 2022, https://www.nytimes.com/interactive /2022/04/18/magazine/julia-roberts-interview.html.

2. Ibid.

3. Ibid.

4. R. E. Lucas et al., "Reexamining Adaptation and the Set Point Model of Happiness: Reactions to Changes in Marital Status," *Journal of Personality and Social Psychology* 84 (3) (2003): 527.

5. Tibor Scitovsky, *The Joyless Economy: The Psychology of Human Satisfaction* (Oxford: Oxford University Press on Demand, 1992), 71.

6. L. H. Epstein et al., "Long-Term Habituation to Food in Obese and Non-obese Women," *American Journal of Clinical Nutrition* 94 (2) (2011): 371–76.

7. R. B. Zajonc, "Feeling and Thinking: Preferences Need No Inference," *American Psychologist* 35 (February 1980): 151–71.

8. L. D. Nelson and T. Meyvis, "Interrupted Consumption: Disrupting Ad-

aptation to Hedonic Experiences," *Journal of Marketing Research* 45 (6) (2008): 654–64.

9. Laurie Santos, "My Life Is Awesome, So Why Can't I Enjoy It?," Aspen Ideas, https://www.aspenideas.org/sessions/my-life-is-awesome-so -why-cant-i-enjoy-it.

10. O. Itkes et al., "Dissociating Affective and Semantic Valence," *Journal of Experimental Psychology: General* 146 (7) (2017): 924.

11. B. Blain and R. B. Rutledge, "Momentary Subjective Well-Being Depends on Learning and Not Reward," *eLife*, November 17, 2020, 9.

12. Oscar Wilde, *The Importance of Being Earnest* (1898), 20.

13. A. Geana et al., "Boredom, Information-Seeking and Exploration," Semantic Scholar, 2016, 6, https://www.semanticscholar.org/paper /Boredom%2C-Information-Seeking-and-Exploration-Geana-Wilson /20851b975b4e2cb99ed2f11cfb2067e10304661b.

14. C. Graham and J. Ruiz Pouel, "Happiness, Stress, and Age: How the U Curve Varies across People and Places," *Journal of Population Economics* 30 (1) (2017): 225–64.

15. Figure adapted from https://www.brookings.edu/articles/happiness -stress-and-age-how-the-u-curve-varies-across-people-and-places/.

16. Graham and Ruiz Pouel, "Happiness, Stress, and Age."

17. National Institute of Mental Health, https://www.nimh.nih.gov/health /statistics/suicide.

18. T. Gilovich, A. Kumar, and L. Jampol, "A Wonderful Life: Experiential Consumption and the Pursuit of Happiness," *Journal of Consumer Psychology* 25 (1) (2015): 152–65.

19. Ibid.

20. *The Works of Samuel Johnson*, LL.D., Volume 1 (New York: George Dearborn, 1837), 412.

21. Ibid.

22. Wilde, *The Importance of Being Earnest*, 6–7.

23. Esther Perel, *Mating in Captivity: Unlocking Erotic Intelligence* (New York: Harper, 2007), 272. We quote from this book at various points below; we spare the reader footnotes for every occasion.

24. Ibid., 10.

25. Ibid.

26. T. K. Shackelford et al., "Absence Makes the Adaptations Grow Fonder: Proportion of Time Apart from Partner, Male Sexual Psychology, and

Sperm Competition in Humans (*Homo sapiens*)," *Journal of Comparative Psychology* 121 (2) (2007): 214.

27. S. Frederick and G. Loewenstein, "Hedonic Adaptation," in *Well-Being: The Foundations of Hedonic Psychology*, ed. Daniel Kahneman, Edward Diener, and Norbert Schwarz (New York: Russell Sage, 1999), 302–29.

28. D. M. Lydon-Staley et al., "Hunters, Busybodies and the Knowledge Network Building Associated with Deprivation Curiosity," *Nature Human Behaviour* 5 (3) (2021): 327–36.

29. Chris Weller, "6 Novels Bill Gates Thinks Everyone Should Read," *Business Insider*, 2017.

30. Tom Popomaronis, "Here's a Full List of Every Book Warren Buffett Has Recommended This Decade—in His Annual Letters," CNBC, 2019.

2: Variety: Why You Should Chop Up the Good but Swallow the Bad Whole

1. James Sudakow, "This Is Why Good Employees Resign within Their First Year and What You Can Do about It," Inc.com, October 18, 2017.

2. Adam Vaccaro, "Why Employees Quit Jobs Right After They've Started," Inc.com, April 17, 2014.

3. E. Diener, R. E. Lucas, and S. Oishi, "Subjective Well-Being: The Science of Happiness and Life Satisfaction," *Handbook of Positive Psychology* 2 (2002): 63–73.

4. E. L. Deci and R. M. Ryan, "Hedonia, Eudaimonia, and Well-Being: An Introduction," *Journal of Happiness Studies* 9 (1) (2008): 1–11.

5. E. O'Brien and S. Kassirer, "People Are Slow to Adapt to the Warm Glow of Giving," *Psychological Science* 30 (2) (2019): 193–204.

6. Ibid.

7. S. Oishi and E. C. Westgate, "A Psychologically Rich Life: Beyond Happiness and Meaning," *Psychological Review* 129 (4) (2022): 790.

8. Ibid.

9. S. D. Levitt, "Heads or Tails: The Impact of a Coin Toss on Major Life Decisions and Subsequent Happiness," *Review of Economic Studies* 88 (1) (2021): 378–405.

10. Ibid.

11. Ibid.

12. L. D. Nelson and T. Meyvis, "Interrupted Consumption: Disrupting Ad-

aptation to Hedonic Experiences," *Journal of Marketing Research* 45 (6) (2008): 654–64.

13. Ibid.

14. Ibid.

15. Ibid.

16. Ibid.

17. Ibid.

18. "New Study Finds What Triggers the 'Holiday Feeling,'" *Travel Bulletin*, 2019, https://www.travelbulletin.co.uk/news-mainmenu/new-study -finds-what-triggers-the-holiday-feeling.

19. Ibid.

3: Social Media: How to Wake Up from a Technologically Induced Coma

1. Tim Harford, "Your Phone's Notification Settings and the Meaning of Life," *Forbes*, 2022.

2. Sam Holstein, "10 Great Ways Quitting Social Media Changed My Life for the Better," https://samholstein.com/10-great-ways-quitting-social-me dia-changed-my-life-for-the-better/.

3. Shovan Chowdhury, "14 Remarkable Ways My Life Changed When I Quit Social Media," Inc.com, September 21, 2017, https://www.inc.com /quora/14-remarkable-ways-my-life-changed-when-i-quit-soc.html.

4. H. Allcott et al., "The Welfare Effects of Social Media," *American Economic Review* 110 (3) (2020): 629–76.

5. R. Zalani, "Screen Time Statistics (2022): Your Smartphone Is Hurting You," Elite Content Marketer.

6. D. Ruby, "Social Media Users—How Many People Use Social Media in 2023," Demand Sage, 2023, https://www.demandsage.com/social-media-users/.

7. Allcott et al., "The Welfare Effects of Social Media."

8. L. Braghieri, R. E. Levy, and A. Makarin, "Social Media and Mental Health," *American Economic Review* 112 (11) (2022): 3660–93.

9. Ibid.

10. Allcott et al., "The Welfare Effects of Social Media."

11. S. Frederick and G. Loewenstein, "Hedonic Adaptation," in *Well-Being: The Foundations of Hedonic Psychology*, ed. Daniel Kahneman, Edward Diener, and Norbert Schwarz (New York: Russell Sage, 1999), 302–29.

12. Ibid.

13. L. H. Bukstel and P. R. Kilmann, "Psychological Effects of Imprisonment on Confined Individuals," *Psychological Bulletin* 88 (2) (1980): 469.

14. Frederick and Loewenstein, "Hedonic Adaptation."

15. T. Wadsworth, "Sex and the Pursuit of Happiness: How Other People's Sex Lives Are Related to Our Sense of Well-Being," *Social Indicators Research* 116 (2014): 115–35.

16. A. Scalia, "The Rule of Law as a Law of Rules," *University of Chicago Law Review* 56 (1989): 1175.

17. Allcott et al., "The Welfare Effects of Social Media," 655.

18. Ibid.

19. Arthur Krieger, "Rethinking Addiction," *Blog of the APA*, April 21, 2022, https://blog.apaonline.org/2022/04/21/rethinking-addiction/; for the original, see Benjamin Rush, *Medical Inquiries and Observations Upon the Diseases of the Mind* (New York: Hafner, 1810), 266.

20. H. Allcott, M. Gentzkow, and L. Song, "Digital Addiction," *American Economic Review* 112 (7) (2022): 2424–63.

21. Ibid.

22. C. Kelly and T. Sharot, "Knowledge-Seeking Reflects and Shapes Mental Health," PsyArXiv, 2023.

23. Chowdhury, "14 Remarkable Ways My Life Changed When I Quit Social Media."

4: Resilience: A Crucial Ingredient for a Healthy Mind

1. Attributed to Michael Rutter 1985, https://medium.com/explore-the-limits/resilience-is-our-ability-to-bounce-back-from-lifes-challenges-and-unforeseen-difficulties-3e99485535a.

2. A. S. Heller, N. I. Kraus, and W. J. Villano, "Depression Is Associated with Blunted Affective Responses to Naturalistic Reward Prediction Error" (in prep).

3. S. Nolen-Hoeksema, B. E. Wisco, and S. Lyubomirsky, "Rethinking Rumination," *Perspectives on Psychological Science* 3 (5) (2008): 400–424.

4. L. K. Globig, B. Blain, and T. Sharot, "When Private Optimism Meets Public Despair: Dissociable Effects on Behavior and Well-Being," *Journal of Risk & Uncertainty* 64 (2022): 1–22.

5. Lara Aknin, Jamil Zaki, and Elizabeth Dunn, "The Pandemic Did Not Affect Mental Health the Way You Think," *Atlantic*, 2021.

6. D. Fancourt et al., "COVID-19 Social Study," *Results Release* 10 (2021): 25.

7. Ibid.

8. R. E. Lucas, A. E. Clark, Y. Georgellis, and E. Diener, "Reexamining Adaptation and the Set Point Model of Happiness: Reactions to Changes in Marital Status," *Journal of Personality and Social Psychology* 84 (3) (2003): 527.

9. K. S. Kendler et al., "A Swedish National Twin Study of Lifetime Major Depression," *American Journal of Psychiatry* 163 (1) (2006): 109–14.

10. D. Cannizzaro, "Return to Normalcy Causing Post-Pandemic Anxiety," Wilx.com, 2021, https://www.wilx.com/2021/06/02/return-to-normalcy -causing-post-pandemic-anxiety/.

11. Upasana Bhat and Tae-jun Kang, "Empress Masako: The Japanese Princess Who Struggles with Royal Life," BBC, 2019.

12. "Adjustment Disorders," Mayo Clinic, 2019, https://www.mayoclinic.org /diseases-conditions/adjustment-disorders/symptoms-causes/syc -20355224.

13. A. Ishai, "Repetition Suppression of Faces Is Modulated by Emotion," *Proceedings of the National Academy of Sciences of the USA* 101 (2004): 9827–32.

14. L. E. Williams et al., "Reduced Habituation in Patients with Schizophrenia," *Schizophrenia Research* 151 (1–3) (2013): 124–32.

15. G. N. Andrade et al., "Atypical Visual and Somatosensory Adaptation in Schizophrenia-Spectrum Disorders," *Translational Psychiatry* 6 (5) (2016): e804.

16. Wikipedia, s.v. "Ornithophobia."

17. J. S. Abramowitz, B. J. Deacon, and S. P. Whiteside, *Exposure Therapy for Anxiety: Principles and Practice* (New York: Guilford, 2019).

5: Creativity: Overcoming the Habituation of Thought

1. C. W. Pollard, *The Soul of the Firm* (Grand Rapids: HarperCollins, 1996), 116.

2. T. Goldman, "High Jumper Dick Fosbury, Who Revolutionized the Sport, with His 'Flop,' Dies at 76," NPR, 2023.

3. Wikipedia, s.v. "Richard Douglas Fosbury."

4. Welch, *The Wizard of Foz: Dick Fosbury's One-Man High-Jump Revolution* (New York: Simon & Schuster, 2018). We quote from this book at various points below; we spare the reader footnotes for every occasion.

5. Ibid.

6. Tower, "Trial and Error: How Dick Fosbury Revolutionized the High Jump," Globalsportsmatters.com, 2018; and "How One Man Changed the High Jump Forever," Olympics, 2018, https://www.youtube.com/watch?v=CZsH46Ek2ao.

7. W. W. Maddux and A. D. Galinsky, "Cultural Borders and Mental Barriers: The Relationship between Living Abroad and Creativity," *Journal of Personality and Social Psychology* 96 (5) (2009): 1047.

8. E. Frith et al., "Systematic Review of the Proposed Associations between Physical Exercise and Creative Thinking," *Europe's Journal of Psychology* 15 (4) (2019): 858.

9. K. J. Main et al., "Change It Up: Inactivity and Repetitive Activity Reduce Creative Thinking," *Journal of Creative Behavior* 54 (2) (2020): 395–406.

10. Ibid.

11. Ibid.

12. Ibid.

13. S. H. Carson, J. B. Peterson, and D. M. Higgins, "Decreased Latent Inhibition Is Associated with Increased Creative Achievement in High-Functioning Individuals," *Journal of Personality and Social Psychology* 85 (3) (2003): 499.

14. Ibid.

15. C. Martindale et al., "Creativity, Oversensitivity, and Rate of Habituation," *Personality and Individual Differences* 20 (4) (1996): 423–27.

16. Carson, Peterson, and Higgins, "Decreased Latent Inhibition Is Associated with Increased Creative Achievement in High-Functioning Individuals."

17. Welch, *The Wizard of Foz.*

18. Richard H. Thaler, convocation address, University of Chicago Graduate School of Business, June 15, 2003.

19. Wikipedia, s.v. "Richard Douglas Fosbury."

20. Ibid.

21. Welch, *The Wizard of Foz.*

6: Lying: How to Keep Your Child from Growing a Long Nose

1. Bonnie Kirchner, *The Bernard Madoff Investment Scam* (Upper Saddle River, NJ: FT Press, 2010).

2. Tali Sharot, "The Danger of Small Lies," Thrive Global, 2022, https://community.thriveglobal.com/the-danger-of-small-lies/.

3. N. Garrett et al., "The Brain Adapts to Dishonesty," *Nature Neuroscience* 19 (12) (2016): 1727–32.

4. D. T. Welsh et al., "The Slippery Slope: How Small Ethical Transgressions Pave the Way for Larger Future Transgressions," *Journal of Applied Psychology*, 100 (1) (2015): 114.

5. H. C. Breiter et al., "Response and Habituation of the Human Amygdala during Visual Processing of Facial Expression," *Neuron* 17 (1996): 875–87; A. Ishai et al., "Repetition Suppression of Faces Is Modulated by Emotion," *Proceedings of the National Academy of Sciences of the USA* 101 (2004): 9827–32; and B. T. Denny et al., "Insula-Amygdala Functional Connectivity Is Correlated with Habituation to Repeated Negative Images," *Social Cognitive and Affective Neuroscience* 9 (2014): 1660–67.

6. P. Dalton, "Olfaction," in *Steven's Handbook of Experimental Psychology: Sensation and Perception*, ed. H. Pashler and S. Yantis (Hoboken, NJ: John Wiley & Sons, 2002), 691–746.

7. S. Schachter and B. Latané, "Crime, Cognition, and the Autonomic Nervous System," in *Nebraska Symposium on Motivation 12*, ed. D. Levine (Lincoln: University of Nebraska, 1964), 221–75.

8. Tali Sharot and Neil Garrett, "Trump's Lying Seems to Be Getting Worse. Psychology Suggests There's a Reason Why," MSNBC, May 23, 2018.

9. K. A. Janezic and A. Gallego, "Eliciting Preferences for Truth-Telling in a Survey of Politicians," *Proceedings of the National Academy of Sciences of the USA* 117 (36) (2020): 22002–8.

10. Jennifer Graham, "Americans Are Increasingly Comfortable with Many White Lies, New Poll Reveals," *Deseret News*, March 28, 2018.

11. Welsh et al., "The Slippery Slope."

12. Clair Weaver, "Belle Gibson: The Girl Who Conned Us All," *Australian Women's Weekly*, June 25, 2015.

13. Melissa Davey, "'None of It's True': Wellness Blogger Belle Gibson Admits She Never Had Cancer," *Guardian*, April 22, 2015.

14. We note that there is strong evidence suggesting that some behavioral scientists who work on dishonesty have also fabricated data.

15. Kirchner, *The Bernard Madoff Investment Scam*.

16. Ibid.

17. J. Graham, J. Haidt, and B. A. Nosek, "Liberals and Conservatives Rely on Different Sets of Moral Foundations," *Journal of Personality and Social Psychology* 96 (5) (2009): 1029.

18. J. Baron and M. Spranca, "Protected Values," *Organizational Behavior and Human Decision Processes* 70 (1) (1997): 1–16; and A. P. McGraw and P. E. Tetlock, "Taboo Trade-Offs, Relational Framing, and the Acceptability of Exchanges," *Journal of Consumer Psychology* 15 (1) (2005): 2–15.

19. *Haaretz*, https://www.haaretz.co.il/gallery/galleryfriday/2022-06-09/ty-article-magazine/.highlight/00000181-3e90-d207-a795-7ef0418c0000.

20. Bernard Williams, *Moral Luck: Philosophical Papers, 1973–1980* (Cambridge: Cambridge University Press, 1981), 18.

21. Sharot, Garrett, and Lazzaro, unpublished article.

7: (Mis)Information: How to Make People Believe (Almost) Anything

1. Adolf Hitler, *Mein Kampf: Zwei Bände in einem Band* (Berlin: Franz Eher Nachfolger, 1943).

2. L. Hasher, D. Goldstein, and T. Toppino, "Frequency and the Conference of Referential Validity," *Journal of Verbal Learning and Verbal Behavior* 16 (1) (1977): 107–12.

3. Ibid.

4. A. Hassan and S. J. Barber, "The Effects of Repetition Frequency on the Illusory Truth Effect," *Cognitive Research: Principles and Implications* 6 (1) (2021): 1–12.

5. G. Pennycook, T. D. Cannon, and D. G. Rand, "Prior Exposure Increases Perceived Accuracy of Fake News," *Journal of Experimental Psychology: General* 147 (12) (2018): 1865.

6. L. K. Fazio et al., "Knowledge Does Not Protect against Illusory Truth," *Journal of Experimental Psychology: General* 144 (5) (2015): 993.

7. J. De Keersmaecker et al., "Investigating the Robustness of the Illusory Truth Effect across Individual Differences in Cognitive Ability, Need for

Cognitive Closure, and Cognitive Style," *Personality and Social Psychology Bulletin* 46 (2) (2020): 204–15.

8. Ibid.

9. J. P. Mitchell et al., "Misattribution Errors in Alzheimer's Disease: The Illusory Truth Effect," *Neuropsychology* 20 (2) (2006): 185.

10. T. R. Levine et al., "Norms, Expectations, and Deception: A Norm Violation Model of Veracity Judgments," *Communications Monographs* 67 (2) (2000): 123–37.

11. D. L. Schacter, "The Seven Sins of Memory: Insights from Psychology and Cognitive Neuroscience," *American Psychologist* 54 (3) (1999): 182.

12. I. Begg, V. Armour, and T. Kerr, "On Believing What We Remember," *Canadian Journal of Behavioural Science / Revue canadienne des sciences du comportement* 17 (3) (1985): 199.

13. K. Fiedler, "Metacognitive Myopia—Gullibility as a Major Obstacle in the Way of Irrational Behavior," in *The Social Psychology of Gullibility: Fake News, Conspiracy Theories, and Irrational Beliefs*, ed. Joseph P. Forgas and Roy Baumeister (New York: Routledge, 2019), 123–39.

14. A. J. Horner and R. N. Henson, "Priming, Response Learning and Repetition Suppression," *Neuropsychologia* 46 (7) (2008): 1979–91.

15. R. Reber and N. Schwarz, "Effects of Perceptual Fluency on Judgments of Truth," *Consciousness and Cognition* 8 (3) (1999): 338–42.

16. Hitler, *Mein Kampf.*

17. V. Vellani et al., "The Illusory Truth Effect Leads to the Spread of Misinformation," *Cognition* 236 (2023): 105421.

18. Barbara Mikkelson, "Leper in Chesterfield Cigarette Factory," Snopes, December 17, 1999, https://www.snopes.com/fact-check/the-leper-who-changes-spots/.

19. I. Skurnik et al., "How Warnings about False Claims Become Recommendations," *Journal of Consumer Research* 31 (4) (2005): 713–24.

20. Ibid.

21. M. Pantazi, O. Klein, and M. Kissine, "Is Justice Blind or Myopic? An Examination of the Effects of Meta-Cognitive Myopia and Truth Bias on Mock Jurors and Judges," *Judgment and Decision Making* 15 (2) (2020): 214.

22. G. Pennycook et al., "Shifting Attention to Accuracy Can Reduce Misinformation Online," *Nature* 592 (7855) (2021): 590–95.

23. T. Sharot, "To Quell Misinformation, Use Carrots—Not Just Sticks," *Nature* 591 (7850) (2021): 347.

24. L. K. Globig, N. Holtz, and T. Sharot, "Changing the Incentive Structure of Social Media Platforms to Halt the Spread of Misinformation," *eLife* 12 (2023): e85767.

8: Risk: What the Swedes Taught Us on Högertrafikomläggningen

1. Mark Synnott, "Legendary Climber Alex Honnold Shares His Closest Call," *National Geographic*, December 30, 2015, https://www.national geographic.com/adventure/article/ropeless-climber-alex-honnolds -closest-call.

2. "Magician Killed Attempting Coffin Escape Trick," *Los Angeles Times*, November 1, 1990; and "When Magic Kills the Magician," *Jon Finch* (blog), https://www.finchmagician.com/blog/when-magic-kills-the-magician.

3. "Magician Dies in Halloween Houdini-Type Stunt," United Press International, November 1, 1990, https://www.upi.com/Archives/1990/11/01 /Magician-dies-in-Halloween-Houdini-type-stunt/2524657435600/.

4. Ibid.

5. Donald S. Bosch, "Risk Habituation," Headington Institute, 2016, https: //www.headington-institute.org/resource/risk-habituation/.

6. H. Haj Ali, M. Glickman, and T. Sharot, "Slippery Slope of Risk-Taking: The Role of Habituation in Risk-Taking Escalation," Computational Cognitive Neuroscience Annual Meeting, 2023.

7. G. F. Loewenstein et al., "Risk as Feelings," *Psychological Bulletin* 127 (2) (2001): 267.

8. Ian Kershaw et al., "David Cameron's Legacy: The Historians' Verdict," *Guardian*, July 15, 2016, https://www.theguardian.com/politics/2016 /jul/15/david-camerons-legacy-the-historians-verdict.

9. L. K. Globig, B. Blain, and T. Sharot, "Perceptions of Personal and Public Risk: Dissociable Effects on Behavior and Well-Being," *Journal of Risk and Uncertainty* 64 (2022): 213–34.

10. P. Slovic, "Perception of Risk," *Science* 236 (4799) (1987): 280–85.

11. J. E. Corter and Y. J. Chen, "Do Investment Risk Tolerance Attitudes Predict Portfolio Risk?," *Journal of Business and Psychology* 20 (3) (2006): 369–81.

12. "Why Workplace Accidents Often Happen Late in Projects," ISHN, October 1, 2016, https://www.ishn.com/articles/104925-why-workplace-accidents -often-happen-late-in-projects.

13. Neil Swidey, *Trapped Under the Sea: One Engineering Marvel, Five Men, and a Disaster Ten Miles into the Darkness* (New York: Crown, 2014).

14. Juni Daalmans, *Human Behavior in Hazardous Situations: Best Practice Safety Management in the Chemical and Process Industries* (Oxford, UK: Butterworth-Heinemann, 2012).

15. Ibid.

16. "Switch to the Right," *Time*, 1967; "Swedish Motorists Move to Right," *Montreal Gazette*, 1967; and Wikipedia, s.v. "Dagen H."

17. C. Perakslis, "Dagen Hogertrafik (H-Day) and Risk Habituation [Last Word]," *IEEE Technology and Society Magazine* 35 (1) (2016): 88.

18. "Cigarette Labeling and Health Warning Requirements," FDA, https://www.fda.gov/tobacco-products/labeling-and-warning-statements-tobacco-products/cigarette-labeling-and-health-warning-requirements.

19. B. B. Anderson et al., "How Polymorphic Warnings Reduce Habituation in the Brain: Insights from an fMRI Study," *Proceedings of the 33rd Annual ACM Conference on Human Factors in Computing Systems*, 2015, 2883–92.

20. A. Vance et al., "Tuning Out Security Warnings: A Longitudinal Examination of Habituation through fMRI, Eye Tracking, and Field Experiments," *MIS Quarterly* 42 (2) (2018): 355–80.

21. Ibid.

22. N. Kim and C. R. Ahn, "Using a Virtual Reality–Based Experiment Environment to Examine Risk Habituation in Construction Safety," *Proceedings of the International Symposium on Automation and Robotics in Construction* (IAARC), 2020.

23. Haj Ali, Glickman, and Sharot, "Slippery Slope of Risk-Taking."

24. "Mortality among Teenagers Aged 12–19 Years: United States, 1999–2006," NCHS Data Brief no. 37, May 2010; and "CDC Childhood Injury Report," 2008.

25. Synnott, "Legendary Climber Alex Honnold Shares His Closest Call."

9: Environment: You Could Live Next to a Pig Farm in the South during Summer

1. René Dubos, "Mere Survival Is Not Enough for Man," *Life*, July 24, 1970, 2.

2. https://www.quora.com/Whats-it-like-to-live-near-train-tracks.

3. https://www.quora.com/How-do-people-who-live-near-the-airport-cope-with-the-noise/answer/Brady-Wade-2.

4. https://libquotes.com/robert-orben/quote/lbw1u0d.

5. https://www.quora.com/How-do-people-who-live-near-the-airport-cope-with-the-noise/answer/Brady-Wade-2.

6. G. W. Evans, S. V. Jacobs, and N. B. Frager, "Adaptation to Air Pollution," *Journal of Environmental Psychology* 2 (2) (1982): 99–108.

7. "Report Says LA Has Most Polluted Air in the US," NBC, 2022.

8. Matthew Taylor and Sandra Laville, "British People Unaware of Pollution Levels in the Air They Breathe—Study," *Guardian*, February 28, 2017.

9. Evans, Jacobs, and Frager, "Adaptation to Air Pollution."

10. Ibid.

11. Sharot Tali, *The Optimism Bias: A Tour of the Irrationally Positive Brain* (New York: Pantheon Books, 2012).

12. L. K. Globig, B. Blain, and T. Sharot, "Perceptions of Personal and Public Risk: Dissociable Effects on Behavior and Well-Being," *Journal of Risk and Uncertainty* 64 (2022): 213–34.

13. R. E. Dunlap, G. H. Gallup Jr., and A. M. Gallup, "Of Global Concern," *Environment Science and Policy for Sustainable Development* 35 (9) (1993): 7–39.

14. A. Levinson, "Happiness and Air Pollution," in *Handbook on Wellbeing, Happiness and the Environment*, ed. David Maddison, Katrin Rehdanz, and Heinz Welsch (Cheltenham, UK: Edward Elgar, 2020), 164–82.

15. Ibid.

16. L. Gunnarsen and P. O. Fanger, "Adaptation to Indoor Air Pollution," *Environment International* 18 (1) (1992): 43–54.

17. Alice Ingall, "Distracted People Can Be 'Smell Blind,'" University of Sussex, June 5, 2018, https://www.sussex.ac.uk/broadcast/read/45089.

18. Y. Shen, S. Dasgupta, and S. Navlakha, "Habituation as a Neural Algorithm for Online Odor Discrimination," *Proceedings of the National Academy of Sciences of the USA* 117 (22) (2020): 12402–10.

19. Friedrich Leopold Goltz, *Beiträge zur Lehre von den Functionen der Nervencentren des Frosches* (Berlin: August Hirschwald, 1869); and James Fallows, "Guest-Post Wisdom on Frogs," *Atlantic*, July 21, 2009, https://www.theatlantic.com/technology/archive/2009/07/guest-post-wisdom-on-frogs/21789/.

20. A. Heinzmann, "Ueber die Wirkung sehr allmäliger Aenderungen thermischer Reize auf die Empfindungsnerven," *Archiv für die gesamte Physiologie des Menschen und der Thiere* 6 (1872): 222–36, https://doi

.org/10.1007/BF01612252; and Edward Wheeler Scripture, *The New Psychology* (New York: W. Scott Publishing, 1897), 300.

21. "Next Time, What Say We Boil a Consultant," *Fast Company*, October 31, 1995; and Whit Gibbons, "The Legend of the Boiling Frog Is Just a Legend," *Ecoviews*, December 23, 2007.

22. Paul Krugman, "Boiling the Frog," *New York Times*, July 13, 2009.

23. Adam Grant, *Think Again: The Power of Knowing What You Don't Know* (New York: Viking, 2021).

24. Fallows, "Guest-Post Wisdom on Frogs."

25. F. C. Moore et al., "Rapidly Declining Remarkability of Temperature Anomalies May Obscure Public Perception of Climate Change," *Proceedings of the National Academy of Sciences of the USA* 116 (11) (2019): 4905–10.

26. Ibid., 4909.

27. T. R. Davis, "Chamber Cold Acclimatization in Man," *Journal of Applied Physiology* 16 (6) (1961): 1011–15.

28. M. Brazaitis et al., "Time Course of Physiological and Psychological Responses in Humans during a 20-Day Severe-Cold-Acclimation Programme," *PLoS One* 9 (4) (2014): e94698.

29. Markham Heid, "How to Help Your Body Adjust to Colder Weather," *Time*, October 29, 2019, https://time.com/5712904/adjust-to-cold-weather/.

30. René Dubos, *So Human an Animal* (New York: Charles Scribner's Sons, 1968).

10: Progress: Breaking the Chains of Low Expectations

1. https://jessepaikin.com/2020/07/05/may-you-always-be-surprised/.

2. https://her-etiquette.com/beautiful-story-start-new-year-jorge-bucay/.

3. B. Stevenson and J. Wolfers, "The Paradox of Declining Female Happiness," *American Economic Journal: Economic Policy* 1 (2) (2009): 190–225.

4. Ibid.

5. C. Tesch-Römer, A. Motel-Klingebiel, and M. J. Tomasik, "Gender Differences in Subjective Well-Being: Comparing Societies with Respect to Gender Equality," *Social Indicators Research* 85 (2) (2008): 329–49; S. Vieira Lima, "A Cross-Country Investigation of the Determinants of the Happiness Gender Gap," chapter 2 in "Essays on Economics and Happiness" (PhD diss., University of Milano-Bicocca, 2013); G. Meisenberg and M. A. Woodley, "Gender Differences in Subjective Well-Being

and Their Relationships with Gender Equality," *Journal of Happiness Studies* 16 (6) (2015): 1539–55; and M. Zuckerman, C. Li, and J. A. Hall, "When Men and Women Differ in Self-Esteem and When They Don't: A Meta-Analysis," *Journal of Research in Personality* 64 (2016): 34–51.

6. https://www.pewresearch.org/social-trends/2023/04/13/in-a-growing-share-of-u-s-marriages-husbands-and-wives-earn-about-the-same/.

7. R. B. Rutledge et al., "A Computational and Neural Model of Momentary Subjective Well-Being," *Proceedings of the National Academy of Sciences of the USA* 111 (33) (2014): 12252–57.

8. C. Graham, "Why Societies Stay Stuck in Bad Equilibrium: Insights from Happiness Studies amidst Prosperity and Adversity," IZA Conference on Frontiers in Labor Economics: The Economics of Well-Being and Happiness, Washington, DC, 2009.

9. Jon Elster, *America before 1787: The Unraveling of a Colonial Regime* (Princeton, NJ: Princeton University Press, 2023).

10. Amartya Sen, *Commodities and Capabilities* (Amsterdam: North-Holland, 1985), 7.

11. Graham, "Why Societies Stay Stuck in Bad Equilibrium."

12. Ibid.

13. Ibid.

14. John F. Helliwell et al., *World Happiness Report 2021*, https://worldhappiness.report/ed/2021/.

15. Elster, *America before 1787*, 45.

16. Graham, "Why Societies Stay Stuck in Bad Equilibrium."

17. Tesch-Römer, Motel-Klingebiel, and Tomasik, "Gender Differences in Subjective Well-Being," and Vieira Lima, "A Cross-Country Investigation of the Determinants of the Happiness Gender Gap."

18. George Orwell, *1984* (Oxford: Oxford University Press, 2021), 208.

11: **Discrimination:** The Gentle Jew, the Miniskirt-Wearing Scientist, and the Children Who Were Just Not Cool

1. John Howard Griffin, *Black Like Me: The Definitive Griffin Estate Edition, Corrected from Original Manuscripts* (Chicago: Wings Press, 2004), 210.

2. Peter Holley, " 'Super Racist' Pool Safety Poster Prompts Red Cross Apology," *Washington Post*, June 27, 2016, https://www.washingtonpost

.com/news/morning-mix/wp/2016/06/27/super-racist-pool-safety-poster-prompts-red-cross-apology/.

3. Ibid.

4. William J. Weatherby and Colin Welland, *Chariots of Fire* (New York: Dell/Quicksilver, 1982), 31.

5. Griffin, *Black Like Me*, 192.

6. Ibid., 49.

7. Ibid., 64.

8. April Dembosky, "Can Virtual Reality Be Used to Combat Racial Bias in Health Care?," KQED, 2021, https://www.kqed.org/news/11898973/can-virtual-reality-help-combat-racial-bias-in-health-care.

9. T. C. Peck et al., "Putting Yourself in the Skin of a Black Avatar Reduces Implicit Racial Bias," *Consciousness and Cognition* 22 (3) (2013): 779–87.

10. Catharine A. MacKinnon, *Sexual Harassment of Working Women: A Case of Sex Discrimination* (New Haven, CT: Yale University Press, 1979).

11. *Meritor Savings Bank v. Vincent*, 477 U.S. 57, 64 (1986) (internal editing symbols omitted).

12. Betty Friedan, *The Feminine Mystique* (New York: W. W. Norton, 2010).

13. Solomon Northup, *Twelve Years a Slave* (Baton Rouge: Louisiana State University Press, 1968).

14. K. Nave et al., "Wilding the Predictive Brain," *Wiley Interdisciplinary Reviews: Cognitive Science* 11 (6) (2020): e1542.

15. X. Ferrer et al., "Bias and Discrimination in AI: A Cross-Disciplinary Perspective," *IEEE Technology and Society Magazine* 40 (2) (2021): 72–80; and K. Miller, "A Matter of Perspective: Discrimination, Bias, and Inequality in AI," in *Legal Regulations, Implications, and Issues Surrounding Digital Data*, ed. Margaret Jackson and Marita Shelly (Hershey, PA: IGI Global, 2020), 182–202.

16. T. Telford, "Apple Card Algorithm Sparks Gender Bias Allegations against Goldman Sachs," *Washington Post*, November 11, 2019, https://www.washingtonpost.com/business/2019/11/11/apple-card-algorithm-sparks-gender-bias-allegations-against-goldman-sachs/.

17. M. Glickman and T. Sharot, "Biased AI Produce Biased Humans," PsyArXiv, 2023.

12: Tyranny: The Devastatingly Incremental Nature of Descent into Fascism

1. Milton Mayer, *They Thought They Were Free* (Chicago: University of Chicago Press, 1955), 168. Several quotations from this book appear below, as will be clear from the context.
2. Sebastian Haffner, *Defying Hitler* (New York: Macmillan, 2000). Here, several quotations from this book appear below, as will be clear from the context; we spare the reader page references.
3. Ibid., 142.
4. Ibid.
5. Mayer, *They Thought They Were Free*, viii.
6. Ibid., 93.
7. Timur Kuran, *Public Truths, Private Lies* (Cambridge, MA: Harvard University Press, 1997), 3.
8. Mayer, *They Thought They Were Free*, 168.
9. Haffner, *Defying Hitler,* 111.
10. Ibid., 150.
11. Ibid., 156.
12. Mayer, *They Thought They Were Free*, 169–70.
13. Haffner, *Defying Hitler*, 85.
14. Stanley Milgram, *Obedience to Authority* (New York: Harper Perennial, 2009).
15. Ibid.
16. S. Milgram, "Behavioral Study of Obedience," *Journal of Abnormal and Social Psychology* 67 (4) (1963): 371–78.
17. J. M. Burger, "Replicating Milgram: Would People Still Obey Today?," *American Psychologist* 64 (1) (2009): 1.

13: Law: Putting a Price on Pain?

1. P. A. Ubel and G. Loewenstein, "Pain and Suffering Awards: They Shouldn't Be (Just) about Pain and Suffering," *Journal of Legal Studies* 37 (S2) (2008): S195–S216.
2. Daniel Kahneman, *Thinking, Fast and Slow* (New York: Farrar, Straus and Giroux, 2011), 402.
3. D. A. Schkade and D. Kahneman, "Does Living in California Make People

Happy? A Focusing Illusion in Judgments of Life Satisfaction," *Psychological Science* 9 (5) (1998): 340–46.

4. *Dauria v. City of New York*, 577 N.Y.S. 2d 64 (N.Y. App. Div. 1991); *Coleman v. Deno*, 832 So. 2d 1016 (La. Ct. App. 2002); *Squibb v. Century Group*, 824 So. 2d 361 (La. Ct. App. 2002); *Thornton v. Amtrak*, 802 So. 2d 816 (La. Ct. App. 2001); and *Keefe v. E & D Specialty Stands, Inc.*, 708 N.Y.S. 2d 214 (N.Y. App. Div. 2000).

5. *Keefe*, 708 N.Y.S. 2d.

6. *Thornton*, 802 So. 2d; see also *Levy v. Bayou Indus. Maint. Servs.*, 855 So. 2d 968 (La. Ct. App. 2003) (awarding $50,000 for loss of enjoyment of life as a result of postconcussion syndrome).

7. *Hatcher v. Ramada Plaza Hotel & Conf. Ctr.*, No. CV010807378S, 2003 WL 430506 (Conn. Super. Ct. Jan. 29, 2003).

8. *Frankel v. Todd*, 260 F. Supp. 772 (E.D. Pa. 1966).

9. *Russo v. Jordan*, No. 27,683 CVN 1998, 2001 WL 914107 (N.Y. Civ. Ct. June 4, 2001).

10. Amartya Sen and Martha Nussbaum have explored the centrality of capabilities in many places. See, for example, Sen, *Commodities and Capabilities*; and Martha Nussbaum, *Creating Capabilities: The Human Development Approach* (Cambridge, MA: Harvard University Press, 2011). We are not using the idea of "capabilities" in the same sense as Sen and Nussbaum, but our use belongs in the same general family, focusing on the capacity to function, rather than subjective mental states.

11. Ubel and Loewenstein, "Pain and Suffering Awards: They Shouldn't Be (Just) about Pain and Suffering."

12. G. Loewenstein and P. A. Ubel, "Hedonic Adaptation and the Role of Decision and Experience Utility in Public Policy," *Journal of Public Economics* 92 (8–9) (2008): 1795–1810.

13. Ibid., 1799.

14. *Matos v. Clarendon Nat. Ins. Co.*, 808 So. 2d 841 (La. Ct. App. 2002).

15. *Daugherty v. Erie R.R. Co.*, 169 A. 2d 549 (Pa. Sup. Ct. 1961).

16. *Nemmers v. United States*, 681 F. Supp. 567 (C.D. Ill. 1988).

17. *Varnell v. Louisiana Tech University*, 709 So. 2d 890, 896 (La. Ct. App. 1998).

14: Experiments in Living: The Future of Dishabituation

1. J. S. Mill, *On Liberty* (London: John W. Parker & Son, 1859), 101.
2. Marco Polo, *The Travels of Marco Polo: The Venetian* (London: J. M. Dent, 1921).
3. John Stuart Mill, *Principles of Political Economy with Some of Their Applications to Social Philosophy*, Volume II (New York: D. Appleton & Company, 1909), 135.
4. Mill, *On Liberty*.
5. H. G. Wells and J. Roberts, *The Island of Dr. Moreau* (Project Gutenberg, 2009), 136.
6. D. E. Levari et al., "Prevalence-Induced Concept Change in Human Judgment," *Science* 360 (6396) (2018): 1465–67.
7. Ibid.
8. Rustichello da Pisa, *The Travels of Marco Polo* (Genoa, n.d., ca. 1300).

INDEX

ABOUT THE AUTHORS

Tali Sharot is a professor of cognitive neuroscience at University College London and MIT. She is the founder and director of the Affective Brain Lab. She has written for outlets including the *New York Times*, *Time*, the *Washington Post*; been a repeat guest on CNN, NBC, MSNBC, and a presenter on the BBC; and served as an adviser for global companies and government projects. Her work has won her prestigious fellowships and prizes from the Wellcome Trust, American Psychological Society, British Psychological Society, and others. Her popular TED Talks have accumulated more than twelve million views. Before becoming a neuroscientist, Sharot worked in the financial industry. She is the author of the award-winning books *The Optimism Bias* and *The Influential Mind*. She lives in Boston and London with her husband and children.

Cass R. Sunstein is the nation's most-cited legal scholar who, for the past fifteen years, has been at the forefront of behavioral economics. From 2009 to 2012, he served as the administrator of the White House Office of Information and Regulatory Affairs. Since that time, he has served in the U.S. government in multiple capacities and worked with the United Nations and the World Health Organization, where he chaired the Technical Advisory Group on Behavioural Insights and Sciences for Health during the COVID-19 pandemic. He is the Robert Walmsley University Professor at Harvard Law School. His book *Nudge*, coauthored with Richard Thaler, was a national bestseller. In 2018, he was the recipient of the Holberg Prize from the government of Norway, sometimes described as the equivalent of the Nobel Prize for law and the humanities. He lives in Concord, Massachusetts, and Washington, DC, with his wife, children, and Labrador Retrievers.